INSIDE GUIDES

AMAZING BUGS

Written by
MIRANDA MACQUITTY

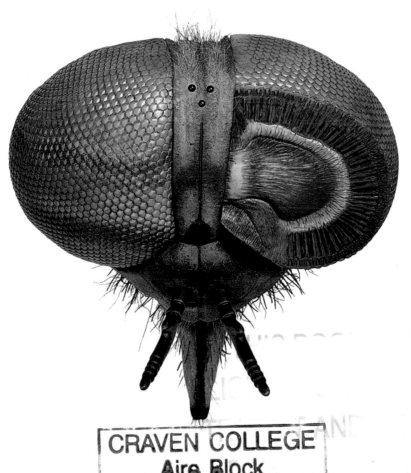

DORLING KINDERSLEY
London • New York • Stuttgart • Moscow

A DORLING KINDERSLEY BOOK

Bees returning
to their hive

Editor Kitty Blount
Art editor Cormac Jordan
Senior art editor Diane Klein
Managing editor Gillian Denton
Managing art editor Julia Harris
Editorial consultant Steven Brooks
Picture research Sam Ruston
Production Charlotte Traill

Photography Andy Crawford, Geoff Brightling
Modelmakers Peter Minister, Gary Staab,
Chris Reynolds and the team at BBC Visual Effects

Bluebottle
feeds on the
remains of
food on a fork

First published in Great Britain
in 1996 by Dorling Kindersley Limited,
9 Henrietta Street, Covent Garden,
London WC2E 8PS

Dissected body
of a shieldbug

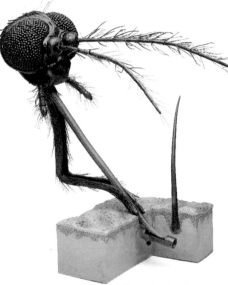

Mosquito feeding
on human blood

A CIP catalogue for this book is available from the British Library.
ISBN 0751 3 54341

Reproduced in Italy by G.R.B. Graphica, Verona
Printed in China by Toppan

Cave-dwelling cricket

Magnified images
of the fruitfly
maggot

A mosquito's
mouthparts

Contents

Model of wasp
showing flight
muscles

Cat flea

Side view of a
desert locust

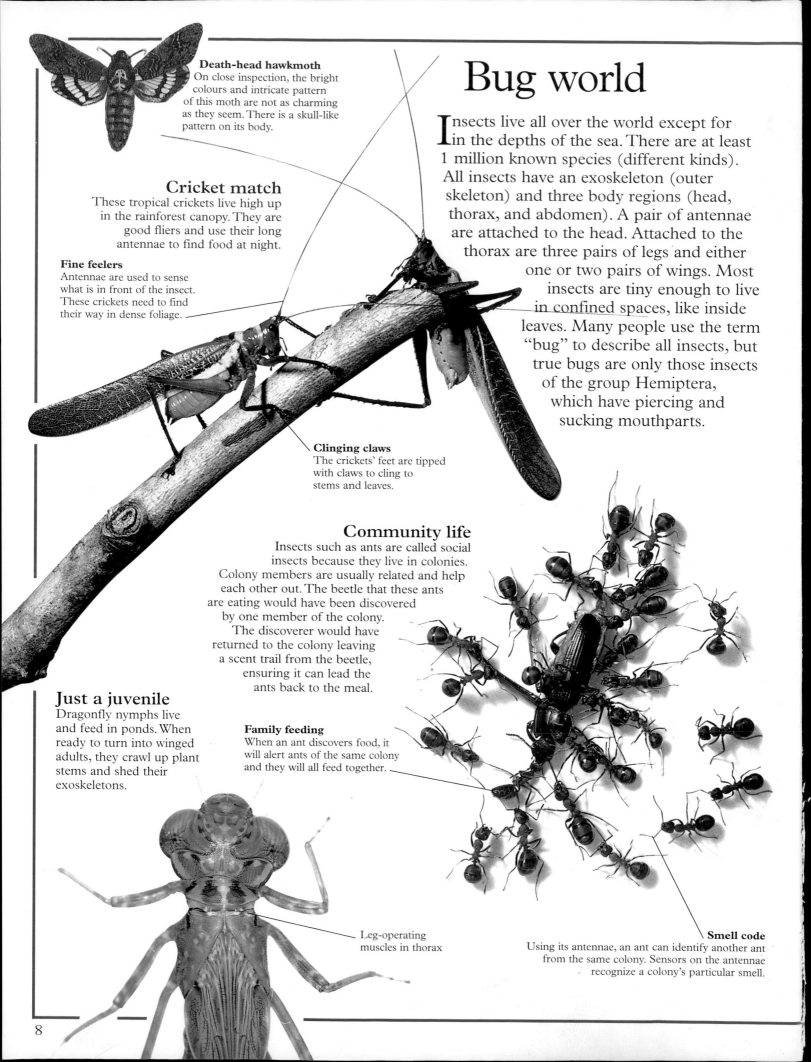

Death-head hawkmoth
On close inspection, the bright colours and intricate pattern of this moth are not as charming as they seem. There is a skull-like pattern on its body.

Bug world

Insects live all over the world except for in the depths of the sea. There are at least 1 million known species (different kinds). All insects have an exoskeleton (outer skeleton) and three body regions (head, thorax, and abdomen). A pair of antennae are attached to the head. Attached to the thorax are three pairs of legs and either one or two pairs of wings. Most insects are tiny enough to live in confined spaces, like inside leaves. Many people use the term "bug" to describe all insects, but true bugs are only those insects of the group Hemiptera, which have piercing and sucking mouthparts.

Cricket match
These tropical crickets live high up in the rainforest canopy. They are good fliers and use their long antennae to find food at night.

Fine feelers
Antennae are used to sense what is in front of the insect. These crickets need to find their way in dense foliage.

Clinging claws
The crickets' feet are tipped with claws to cling to stems and leaves.

Community life
Insects such as ants are called social insects because they live in colonies. Colony members are usually related and help each other out. The beetle that these ants are eating would have been discovered by one member of the colony. The discoverer would have returned to the colony leaving a scent trail from the beetle, ensuring it can lead the ants back to the meal.

Just a juvenile
Dragonfly nymphs live and feed in ponds. When ready to turn into winged adults, they crawl up plant stems and shed their exoskeletons.

Family feeding
When an ant discovers food, it will alert ants of the same colony and they will all feed together.

Leg-operating muscles in thorax

Smell code
Using its antennae, an ant can identify another ant from the same colony. Sensors on the antennae recognize a colony's particular smell.

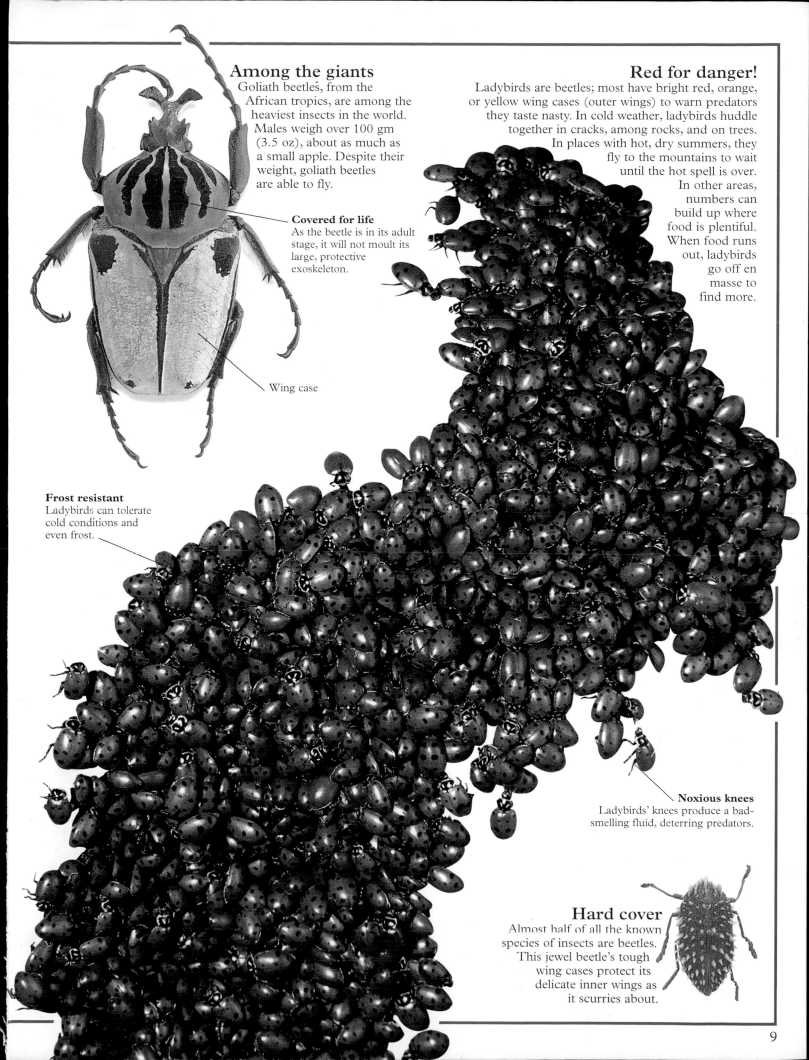

Among the giants

Goliath beetles, from the African tropics, are among the heaviest insects in the world. Males weigh over 100 gm (3.5 oz), about as much as a small apple. Despite their weight, goliath beetles are able to fly.

Covered for life
As the beetle is in its adult stage, it will not moult its large, protective exoskeleton.

Wing case

Red for danger!

Ladybirds are beetles; most have bright red, orange, or yellow wing cases (outer wings) to warn predators they taste nasty. In cold weather, ladybirds huddle together in cracks, among rocks, and on trees. In places with hot, dry summers, they fly to the mountains to wait until the hot spell is over. In other areas, numbers can build up where food is plentiful. When food runs out, ladybirds go off en masse to find more.

Frost resistant
Ladybirds can tolerate cold conditions and even frost.

Noxious knees
Ladybirds' knees produce a bad-smelling fluid, deterring predators.

Hard cover

Almost half of all the known species of insects are beetles. This jewel beetle's tough wing cases protect its delicate inner wings as it scurries about.

Outside an insect

The rhinoceros beetle uses spikes on its body to wrestle other males.

An insect's skeleton, called an exoskeleton, is on the outside, protecting the insect like a suit of armour. The exoskeleton covers the entire body, forming thick protective plates, delicate wings, hairs, and even the eyes' transparent lenses. The exoskeleton is tough, and made mainly of a horny substance, called chitin. The outermost layer is waxy to keep in body moisture. The exoskeleton must be shed for an insect to grow. Before it is moulted, it becomes thinner as the insect absorbs all the goodness from it. The old exoskeleton splits and the next stage emerges with a new exoskeleton. Before this hardens, the insect increases its size by swallowing air or water.

Careful coronet

During the day, the coronet moth rests on the bark of a tree. The moth's mottled colours are good camouflage, so it is less likely to be spotted by predators.

Abdomen
Between each segment of the abdomen is a ring of thinner, more flexible exoskeleton. This allows the abdomen to bend.

Flaps for flying

The wings of any insect are just thin extensions of the exoskeleton. Unlike birds, pterodactyls, and bats, insects did not convert an existing pair of limbs when they evolved wings. So this moth still has two pairs of wings and three pairs of legs.

Shieldbug

The body of a shieldbug is wide and flat. Shieldbugs produce off-putting smells to warn attackers, so they are also known as stinkbugs. The smells are produced by glands in the thorax. In some cases, the smell is strong enough to give a person sniffing a bug a headache. This shieldbug's colours are produced by pigments in the exoskeleton. Some bugs are also iridescent (shiny) due to rays of light being bounced off microscopic layers within the exoskeleton.

Landing platform
This petal looks like a female bumblebee's abdomen.

Eye spots
These may fool a predator into thinking the moth is a larger animal.

Like a bee

The flowers of the bee orchid look like female bumblebees and attract male bumblebees. In attempting to mate with the flower, the male collects pollen on his body. When the frustrated bee attempts to mate with another bee orchid, he pollinates the flower.

Wing scales

The overlapping scales on the wings of a male morpho butterfly, found in South American rainforests, are a brilliant iridescent blue colour. This is produced by light bouncing back from microscopic ridges on the surface and layers within the scales.

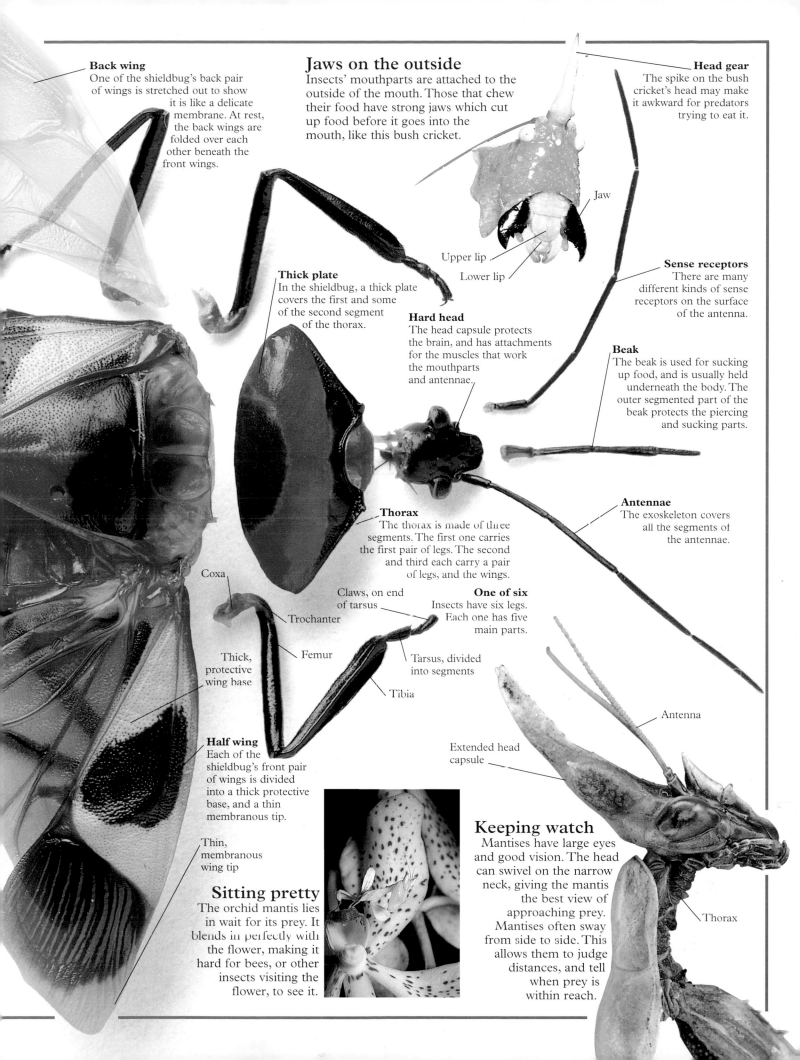

Back wing
One of the shieldbug's back pair
of wings is stretched out to show
it is like a delicate
membrane. At rest,
the back wings are
folded over each
other beneath the
front wings.

Jaws on the outside
Insects' mouthparts are attached to the
outside of the mouth. Those that chew
their food have strong jaws which cut
up food before it goes into the
mouth, like this bush cricket.

Jaw

Upper lip

Lower lip

Head gear
The spike on the bush
cricket's head may make
it awkward for predators
trying to eat it.

Sense receptors
There are many
different kinds of sense
receptors on the surface
of the antenna.

Thick plate
In the shieldbug, a thick plate
covers the first and some
of the second segment
of the thorax.

Hard head
The head capsule protects
the brain, and has attachments
for the muscles that work
the mouthparts
and antennae.

Beak
The beak is used for sucking
up food, and is usually held
underneath the body. The
outer segmented part of the
beak protects the piercing
and sucking parts.

Antennae
The exoskeleton covers
all the segments of
the antennae.

Thorax
The thorax is made of three
segments. The first one carries
the first pair of legs. The second
and third each carry a pair
of legs, and the wings.

Coxa

Trochanter

Thick,
protective
wing base

Femur

Claws, on end
of tarsus

One of six
Insects have six legs.
Each one has five
main parts.

Tarsus, divided
into segments

Tibia

Half wing
Each of the
shieldbug's front pair
of wings is divided
into a thick protective
base, and a thin
membranous tip.

Thin,
membranous
wing tip

Sitting pretty
The orchid mantis lies
in wait for its prey. It
blends in perfectly with
the flower, making it
hard for bees, or other
insects visiting the
flower, to see it.

Antenna

Extended head
capsule

Keeping watch
Mantises have large eyes
and good vision. The head
can swivel on the narrow
neck, giving the mantis
the best view of
approaching prey.
Mantises often sway
from side to side. This
allows them to judge
distances, and tell
when prey is
within reach.

Thorax

Inside an insect

Inside an insect's exoskeleton are its soft body organs. The gut is a long tube where food is digested and then absorbed. Waste collects at the far end of the gut and is passed out through the anus. The digested food is carried to the tissues in the blood, which bathes all the organs. The blood is pumped around by the tube-shaped heart, helped by body movements. Waste is removed from the blood by the malpighian tubules, which act in a similar way to human kidneys. Unlike humans, insects do not have lungs nor does their blood carry oxygen, instead they breathe through tracheae (pp. 18–19). The insect's actions are controlled by the brain and nerve cord.

Skeleton section
The insect exoskeleton is composed of layers, which are produced by an inner sheet of cells.

Diaphragm
This membrane supports the heart. The diaphragm also separates the heart from the blood-filled space that contains the body organs.

Anus, through which waste is excreted

Hindgut with thin lining

Malpighian tubules

Nerve centre
Nerve centres are attached to the nerve cord. They send messages to muscles.

Digestive system
An insect's digestive system, as shown in this model of a locust, divides into three parts; the foregut, from mouth to gizzard; the midgut, from the caecae to the malpighian tubules; and the hindgut. Swallowed plant material is stored in the crop. In the midgut, food is broken down by enzymes and absorbed. The malpighian tubules absorb wastes from the blood. These, as well as food wastes from the midgut, pass into the hindgut to be excreted with the droppings. Water and salts are absorbed from the wastes in the hindgut. The rectum channels waste to the anus.

All aglow
Certain kinds of beetle, such as this click beetle, signal to their mates by giving out flashes of light. The flashes are produced by chemical reactions inside the body. Different species living in the same place use a particular number of flashes to avoid attracting the wrong mate.

X-ray bug
People use x-rays to see the state of their bones. Because insects have the skeleton on the outside, it is hard for x-rays to penetrate their tissues. This x-ray of a cockchafer beetle shows the outline of its jointed legs and its fan-shaped antennae.

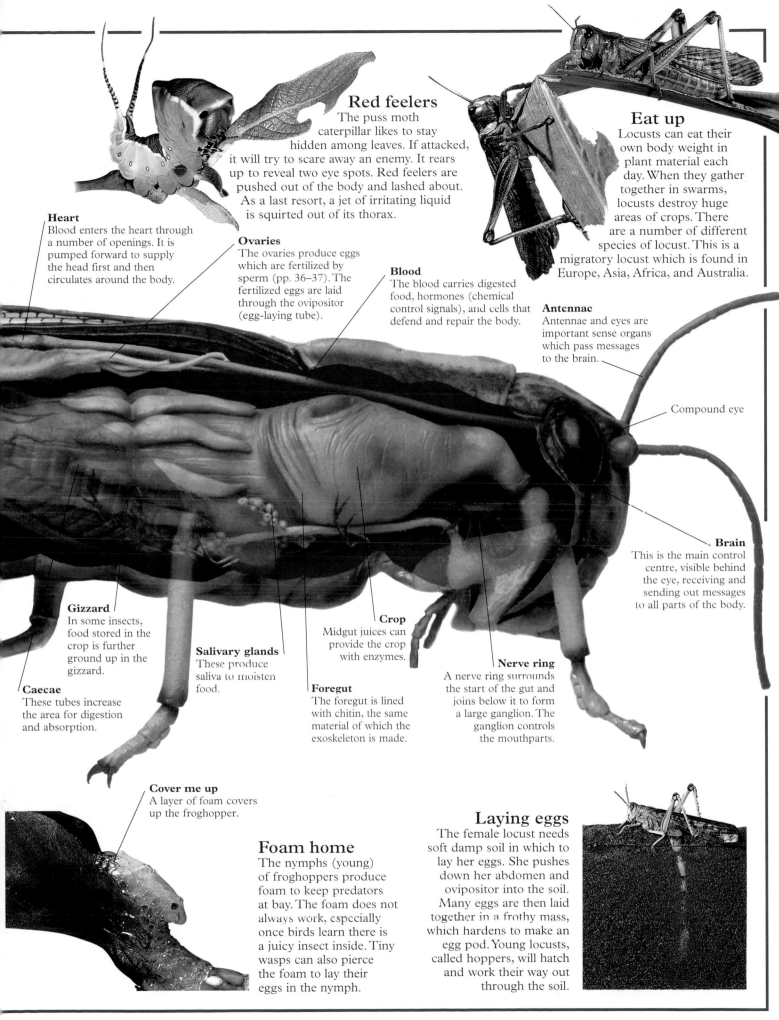

Red feelers

The puss moth caterpillar likes to stay hidden among leaves. If attacked, it will try to scare away an enemy. It rears up to reveal two eye spots. Red feelers are pushed out of the body and lashed about. As a last resort, a jet of irritating liquid is squirted out of its thorax.

Eat up

Locusts can eat their own body weight in plant material each day. When they gather together in swarms, locusts destroy huge areas of crops. There are a number of different species of locust. This is a migratory locust which is found in Europe, Asia, Africa, and Australia.

Heart
Blood enters the heart through a number of openings. It is pumped forward to supply the head first and then circulates around the body.

Ovaries
The ovaries produce eggs which are fertilized by sperm (pp. 36–37). The fertilized eggs are laid through the ovipositor (egg-laying tube).

Blood
The blood carries digested food, hormones (chemical control signals), and cells that defend and repair the body.

Antennae
Antennae and eyes are important sense organs which pass messages to the brain.

Compound eye

Brain
This is the main control centre, visible behind the eye, receiving and sending out messages to all parts of the body.

Gizzard
In some insects, food stored in the crop is further ground up in the gizzard.

Caecae
These tubes increase the area for digestion and absorption.

Salivary glands
These produce saliva to moisten food.

Crop
Midgut juices can provide the crop with enzymes.

Foregut
The foregut is lined with chitin, the same material of which the exoskeleton is made.

Nerve ring
A nerve ring surrounds the start of the gut and joins below it to form a large ganglion. The ganglion controls the mouthparts.

Cover me up
A layer of foam covers up the froghopper.

Foam home

The nymphs (young) of froghoppers produce foam to keep predators at bay. The foam does not always work, especially once birds learn there is a juicy insect inside. Tiny wasps can also pierce the foam to lay their eggs in the nymph.

Laying eggs

The female locust needs soft damp soil in which to lay her eggs. She pushes down her abdomen and ovipositor into the soil. Many eggs are then laid together in a frothy mass, which hardens to make an egg pod. Young locusts, called hoppers, will hatch and work their way out through the soil.

Blood sucker

Mosquitoes use their needle-like mouthparts to pierce human skin and then to suck blood. The itchy "bite" is a reaction to the cocktail of substances which they inject before sucking the blood. This cocktail makes the blood flow more strongly and stops it from clotting. Only female mosquitoes suck blood because it provides them with protein to help develop their eggs. Male mosquitoes take gentle sips of sugary fluids, such as nectar. The female mosquito homes in on humans by sensing the carbon dioxide breathed out. When it lands, the mouthparts probe the skin for a blood capillary. Certain kinds of female mosquitoes can be deadly because they pass a disease to their hosts. This disease, malaria, is caused by a microscopic parasite and kills up to 2 million people each year. The parasite is picked up when the mosquito feeds on an infected person. It is passed on as the mosquito injects saliva into another person. Other blood-sucking insects, such as tsetse flies, also transmit diseases.

Male mosquito
Unlike the female mosquito, the male does not suck blood.

Nasty disease
This kissing bug's "bite" transmits a nasty disease as well as leaving an itchy swelling.

Kissing bug
This tropical American bug is called a kissing bug because it "bites" people's faces. It carries the parasite that causes a fever called Chagas' disease. The parasite is passed in the bug's droppings after it has fed on blood. A person scratching the bite then introduces the parasite into the wound.

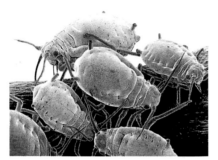

Sap suckers
Aphids suck sap from plants. Their mouthparts pierce the leaf surface and a tube is thrust inside. Sap-digesting saliva is carried into the leaf and digested sap is then sucked up.

Food canal
Human blood is sucked up through this canal into the mosquito.

Mandible
The sharp points of the mandibles break the surface of the host's skin.

Protective sheath

Bad bite
Blackflies have irritating "bites" for both people and livestock. Plagues of blackflies can kill cattle and horses by poisoning their blood.

Maxilla
The serrated edges cut through the skin.

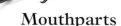

Mouthparts
When not in use, the mosquito's piercing and sucking mouthparts are held safe within the protective sheath. The piercing mandibles and maxillae are sometimes called the "stylets".

Hypopharynx
The salivary duct runs down the hypopharynx carrying substances that encourage the blood to flow.

Not just us
There are over 3,000 kinds of mosquito. The females of most suck blood. Besides humans, mosquitoes feed on rabbits, cattle, birds, and snakes. Even mudskipper fish, when resting on mud, are prey to mosquitoes.

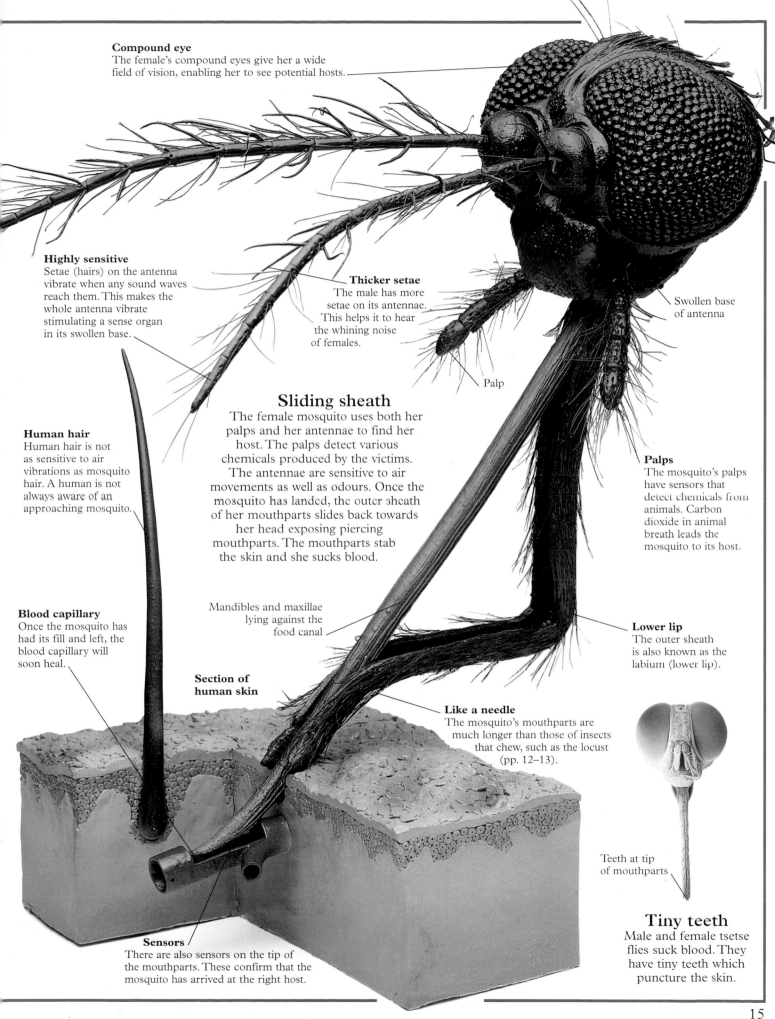

Compound eye
The female's compound eyes give her a wide field of vision, enabling her to see potential hosts.

Highly sensitive
Setae (hairs) on the antenna vibrate when any sound waves reach them. This makes the whole antenna vibrate stimulating a sense organ in its swollen base.

Thicker setae
The male has more setae on its antennae. This helps it to hear the whining noise of females.

Palp

Swollen base of antenna

Sliding sheath
The female mosquito uses both her palps and her antennae to find her host. The palps detect various chemicals produced by the victims. The antennae are sensitive to air movements as well as odours. Once the mosquito has landed, the outer sheath of her mouthparts slides back towards her head exposing piercing mouthparts. The mouthparts stab the skin and she sucks blood.

Human hair
Human hair is not as sensitive to air vibrations as mosquito hair. A human is not always aware of an approaching mosquito.

Palps
The mosquito's palps have sensors that detect chemicals from animals. Carbon dioxide in animal breath leads the mosquito to its host.

Blood capillary
Once the mosquito has had its fill and left, the blood capillary will soon heal.

Mandibles and maxillae lying against the food canal

Lower lip
The outer sheath is also known as the labium (lower lip).

Section of human skin

Like a needle
The mosquito's mouthparts are much longer than those of insects that chew, such as the locust (pp. 12–13).

Teeth at tip of mouthparts

Sensors
There are also sensors on the tip of the mouthparts. These confirm that the mosquito has arrived at the right host.

Tiny teeth
Male and female tsetse flies suck blood. They have tiny teeth which puncture the skin.

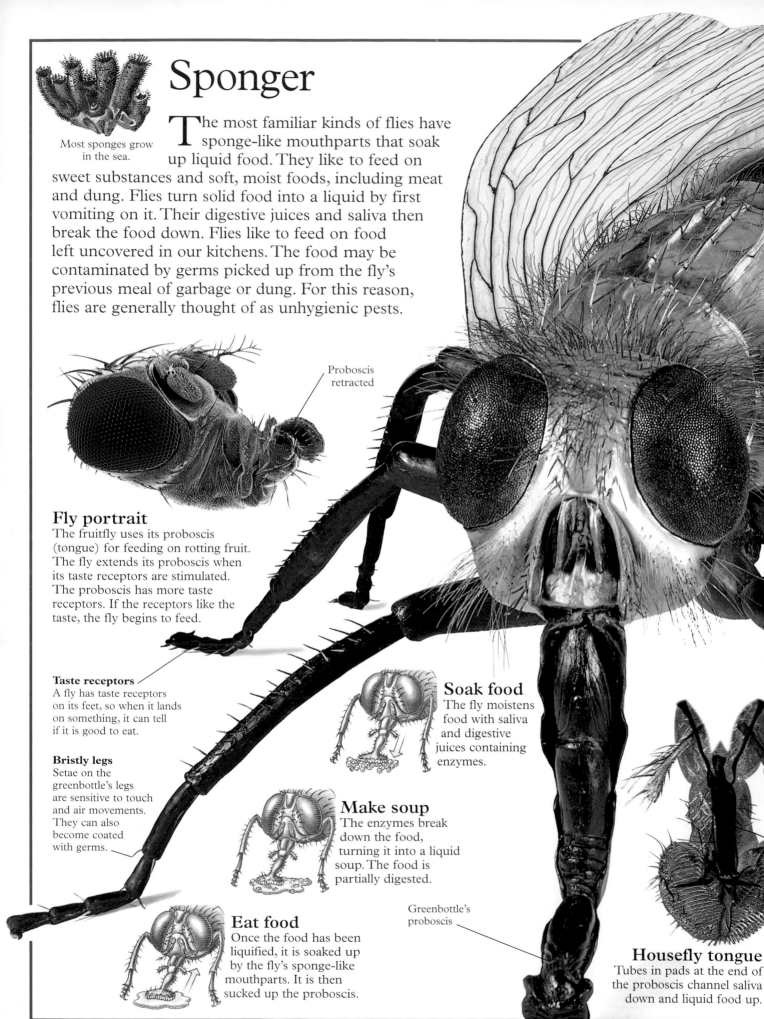

Sponger

Most sponges grow in the sea.

The most familiar kinds of flies have sponge-like mouthparts that soak up liquid food. They like to feed on sweet substances and soft, moist foods, including meat and dung. Flies turn solid food into a liquid by first vomiting on it. Their digestive juices and saliva then break the food down. Flies like to feed on food left uncovered in our kitchens. The food may be contaminated by germs picked up from the fly's previous meal of garbage or dung. For this reason, flies are generally thought of as unhygienic pests.

Proboscis retracted

Fly portrait
The fruitfly uses its proboscis (tongue) for feeding on rotting fruit. The fly extends its proboscis when its taste receptors are stimulated. The proboscis has more taste receptors. If the receptors like the taste, the fly begins to feed.

Taste receptors
A fly has taste receptors on its feet, so when it lands on something, it can tell if it is good to eat.

Bristly legs
Setae on the greenbottle's legs are sensitive to touch and air movements. They can also become coated with germs.

Soak food
The fly moistens food with saliva and digestive juices containing enzymes.

Make soup
The enzymes break down the food, turning it into a liquid soup. The food is partially digested.

Eat food
Once the food has been liquified, it is soaked up by the fly's sponge-like mouthparts. It is then sucked up the proboscis.

Greenbottle's proboscis

Housefly tongue
Tubes in pads at the end of the proboscis channel saliva down and liquid food up.

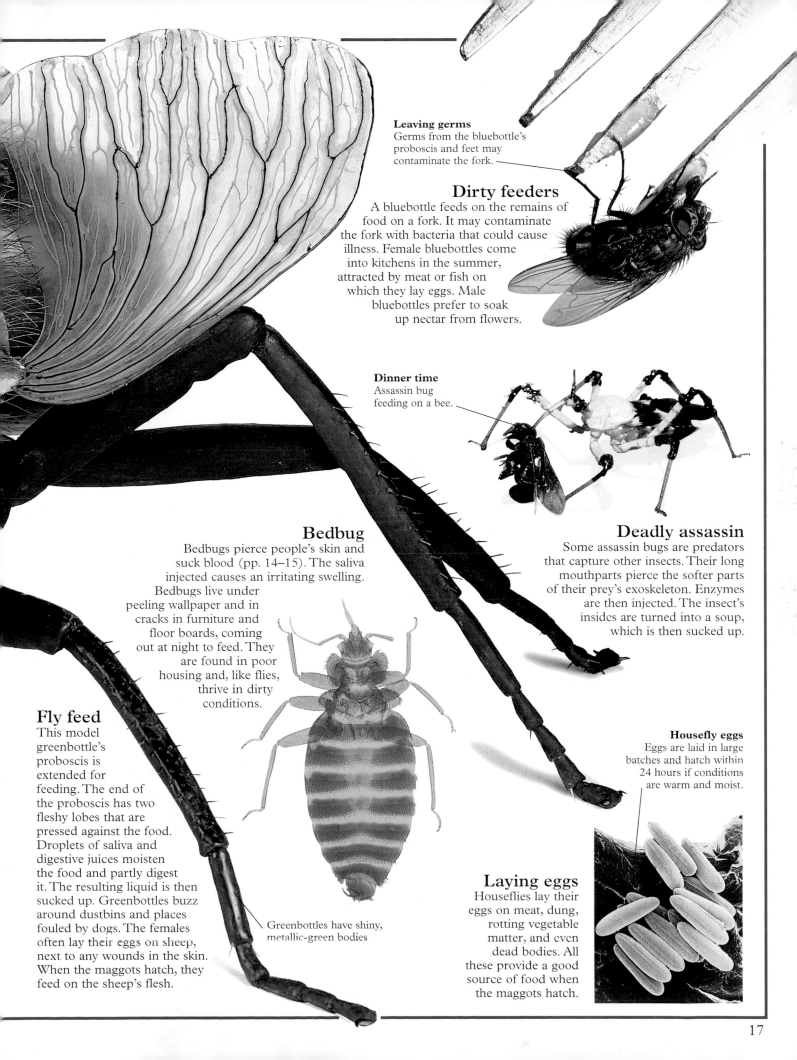

Leaving germs
Germs from the bluebottle's proboscis and feet may contaminate the fork.

Dirty feeders
A bluebottle feeds on the remains of food on a fork. It may contaminate the fork with bacteria that could cause illness. Female bluebottles come into kitchens in the summer, attracted by meat or fish on which they lay eggs. Male bluebottles prefer to soak up nectar from flowers.

Dinner time
Assassin bug feeding on a bee.

Deadly assassin
Some assassin bugs are predators that capture other insects. Their long mouthparts pierce the softer parts of their prey's exoskeleton. Enzymes are then injected. The insect's insides are turned into a soup, which is then sucked up.

Bedbug
Bedbugs pierce people's skin and suck blood (pp. 14–15). The saliva injected causes an irritating swelling. Bedbugs live under peeling wallpaper and in cracks in furniture and floor boards, coming out at night to feed. They are found in poor housing and, like flies, thrive in dirty conditions.

Fly feed
This model greenbottle's proboscis is extended for feeding. The end of the proboscis has two fleshy lobes that are pressed against the food. Droplets of saliva and digestive juices moisten the food and partly digest it. The resulting liquid is then sucked up. Greenbottles buzz around dustbins and places fouled by dogs. The females often lay their eggs on sheep, next to any wounds in the skin. When the maggots hatch, they feed on the sheep's flesh.

Greenbottles have shiny, metallic-green bodies

Housefly eggs
Eggs are laid in large batches and hatch within 24 hours if conditions are warm and moist.

Laying eggs
Houseflies lay their eggs on meat, dung, rotting vegetable matter, and even dead bodies. All these provide a good source of food when the maggots hatch.

Breathing holes

Insects breathe by taking in air, containing oxygen, through a series of holes, called spiracles. Spiracles are found along each side of the body. They can be opened and closed to control the passage of air in and out. The spiracles are connected to a series of branching tubes, called tracheae. These divide into finer branches that take oxygen to all the tissues. Most of the waste gas from respiration, carbon dioxide, passes through the tracheae and out of the spiracles. Some carbon dioxide is also lost through the body surface. Active insects have air sacs connected to the tracheae. Body movements help squeeze air in and out of these sacs. In this way, enough oxygen reaches the hard-working muscles. When an insect moults its exoskeleton, it must also shed its tracheae because they are connected to the exoskeleton.

Caterpillar
The spiracles of the peacock moth caterpillar look like orange ovals when closed.

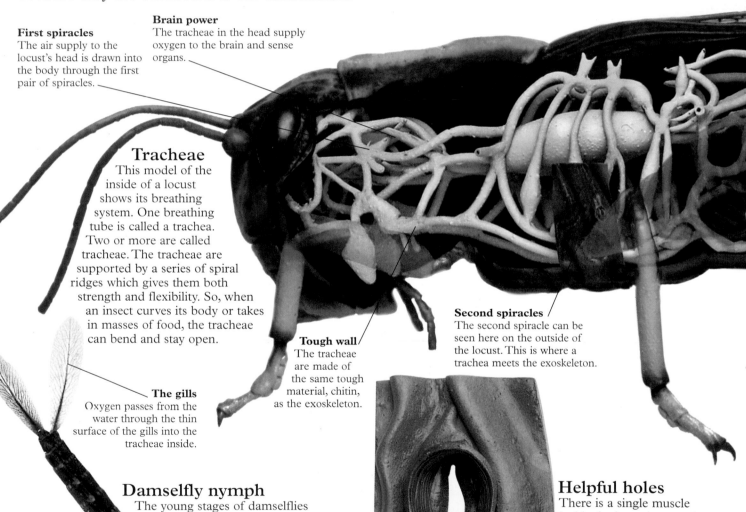

First spiracles
The air supply to the locust's head is drawn into the body through the first pair of spiracles.

Brain power
The tracheae in the head supply oxygen to the brain and sense organs.

Tracheae
This model of the inside of a locust shows its breathing system. One breathing tube is called a trachea. Two or more are called tracheae. The tracheae are supported by a series of spiral ridges which gives them both strength and flexibility. So, when an insect curves its body or takes in masses of food, the tracheae can bend and stay open.

The gills
Oxygen passes from the water through the thin surface of the gills into the tracheae inside.

Tough wall
The tracheae are made of the same tough material, chitin, as the exoskeleton.

Second spiracles
The second spiracle can be seen here on the outside of the locust. This is where a trachea meets the exoskeleton.

Damselfly nymph
The young stages of damselflies are called nymphs and live in fresh water. They breathe through a set of three gills at the tip of the abdomen.

Wing buds
Long wing buds show this is a mature nymph.

Helpful holes
There is a single muscle inside the locust's second spiracle which keeps the lips together and the spiracle closed. When the muscle relaxes, the lips spring apart and the spiracle opens. Other spiracles can have two sets of muscles, one for opening and the other for closing. Being able to close the spiracles helps stop loss of body moisture. This is especially important for insects that live in dry places.

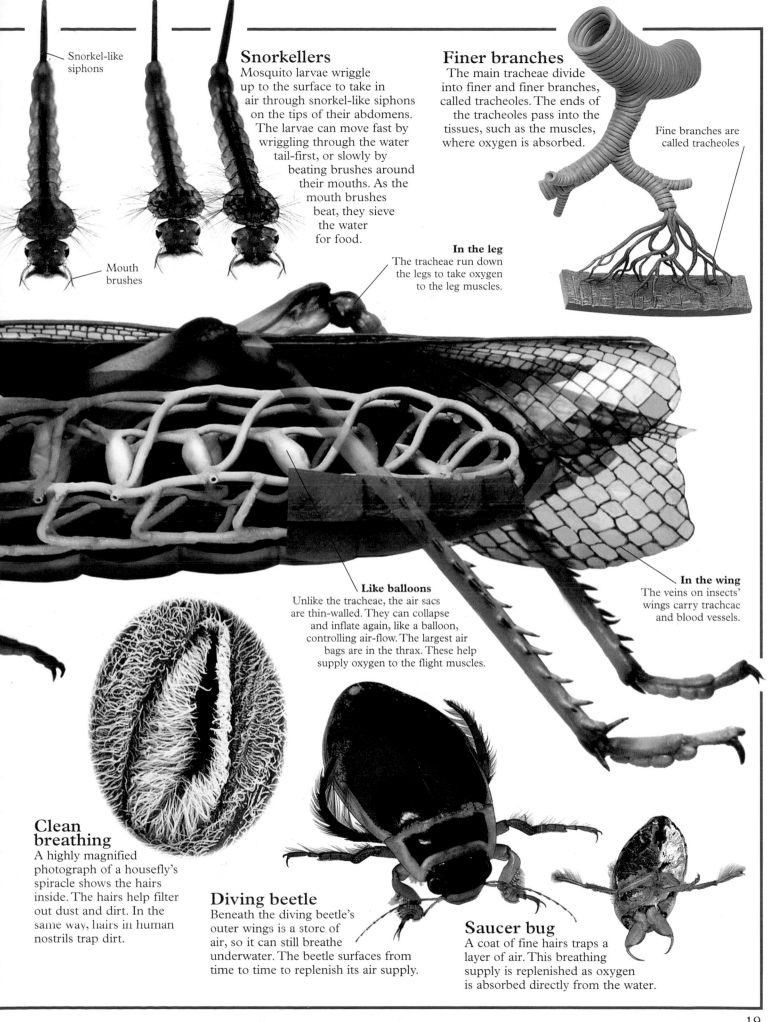

Snorkel-like
siphons

Mouth
brushes

Snorkellers

Mosquito larvae wriggle
up to the surface to take in
air through snorkel-like siphons
on the tips of their abdomens.
The larvae can move fast by
wriggling through the water
tail-first, or slowly by
beating brushes around
their mouths. As the
mouth brushes
beat, they sieve
the water
for food.

Finer branches

The main tracheae divide
into finer and finer branches,
called tracheoles. The ends of
the tracheoles pass into the
tissues, such as the muscles,
where oxygen is absorbed.

Fine branches are
called tracheoles

In the leg
The tracheae run down
the legs to take oxygen
to the leg muscles.

In the wing
The veins on insects'
wings carry trachcac
and blood vessels.

Like balloons
Unlike the tracheae, the air sacs
are thin-walled. They can collapse
and inflate again, like a balloon,
controlling air-flow. The largest air
bags are in the thrax. These help
supply oxygen to the flight muscles.

Clean
breathing

A highly magnified
photograph of a housefly's
spiracle shows the hairs
inside. The hairs help filter
out dust and dirt. In the
same way, hairs in human
nostrils trap dirt.

Diving beetle

Beneath the diving beetle's
outer wings is a store of
air, so it can still breathe
underwater. The beetle surfaces from
time to time to replenish its air supply.

Saucer bug

A coat of fine hairs traps a
layer of air. This breathing
supply is replenished as oxygen
is absorbed directly from the water.

Bug-eyed

Insects' large, bulging eyes, like the eyes in this model of a horsefly's head, can seem creepy. They are very different from human eyes. Insects have compound eyes composed of many tiny eyelets (ommatidia). The more important sight is to an insect, the larger the eyes and the more eyelets it has. The female horsefly, for example, needs good eyesight to see the animals and people from whom she sucks blood. Each eyelet picks up only part of the field of vision. The individual signals are probably interpreted by the brain as a mosaic image. This type of eye is good at detecting movement because different eyelets are stimulated as something moves across the insect's vision.

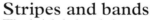

Six-sided lens
Light enters each eyelet through these lenses.

Horsefly
Both male and female horseflies have large, iridescent compound eyes. Only the females suck blood. The males use their eyes to help them find sugary substances on which to feed.

Stripes and bands
The brightly banded pattern on a horsefly's compound eye is due to light waves bouncing off the surface of the lenses. In doing so, some light waves are cancelled out and others enhanced. This phenomenon is known as interference. Grasshoppers and dragonflies have stripes and spots on their eyes. This is due to different concentrations of pigments in the cells surrounding the cone-shaped lenses.

Eye protectors
A robberfly catches insect prey in mid-air. The hairs on its face help protect its eyes from the struggling victim.

All round vision
A dragonfly has large compound eyes that meet on top of its head. It can see above, below, sideways, and behind as it flies along.

Far apart
The widely spaced eyes of this damselfly help it to judge distances. The head can also be rotated on its narrow neck.

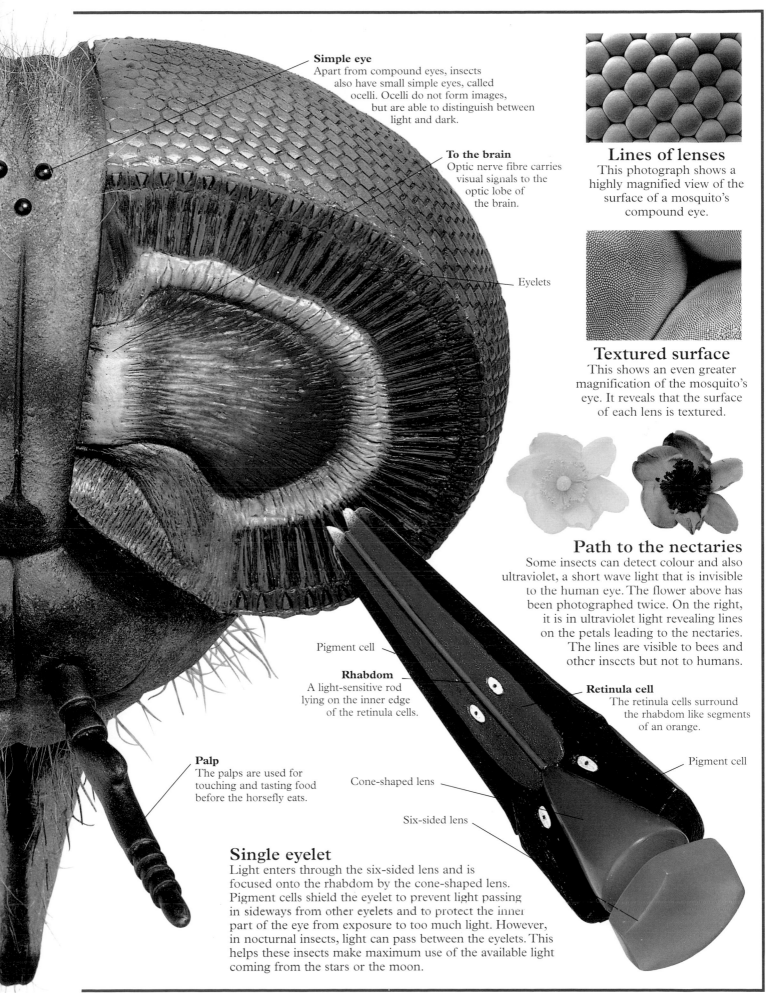

Simple eye
Apart from compound eyes, insects also have small simple eyes, called ocelli. Ocelli do not form images, but are able to distinguish between light and dark.

To the brain
Optic nerve fibre carries visual signals to the optic lobe of the brain.

Eyelets

Lines of lenses
This photograph shows a highly magnified view of the surface of a mosquito's compound eye.

Textured surface
This shows an even greater magnification of the mosquito's eye. It reveals that the surface of each lens is textured.

Path to the nectaries
Some insects can detect colour and also ultraviolet, a short wave light that is invisible to the human eye. The flower above has been photographed twice. On the right, it is in ultraviolet light revealing lines on the petals leading to the nectaries. The lines are visible to bees and other insects but not to humans.

Pigment cell

Rhabdom
A light-sensitive rod lying on the inner edge of the retinula cells.

Retinula cell
The retinula cells surround the rhabdom like segments of an orange.

Pigment cell

Palp
The palps are used for touching and tasting food before the horsefly eats.

Cone-shaped lens

Six-sided lens

Single eyelet
Light enters through the six-sided lens and is focused onto the rhabdom by the cone-shaped lens. Pigment cells shield the eyelet to prevent light passing in sideways from other eyelets and to protect the inner part of the eye from exposure to too much light. However, in nocturnal insects, light can pass between the eyelets. This helps these insects make maximum use of the available light coming from the stars or the moon.

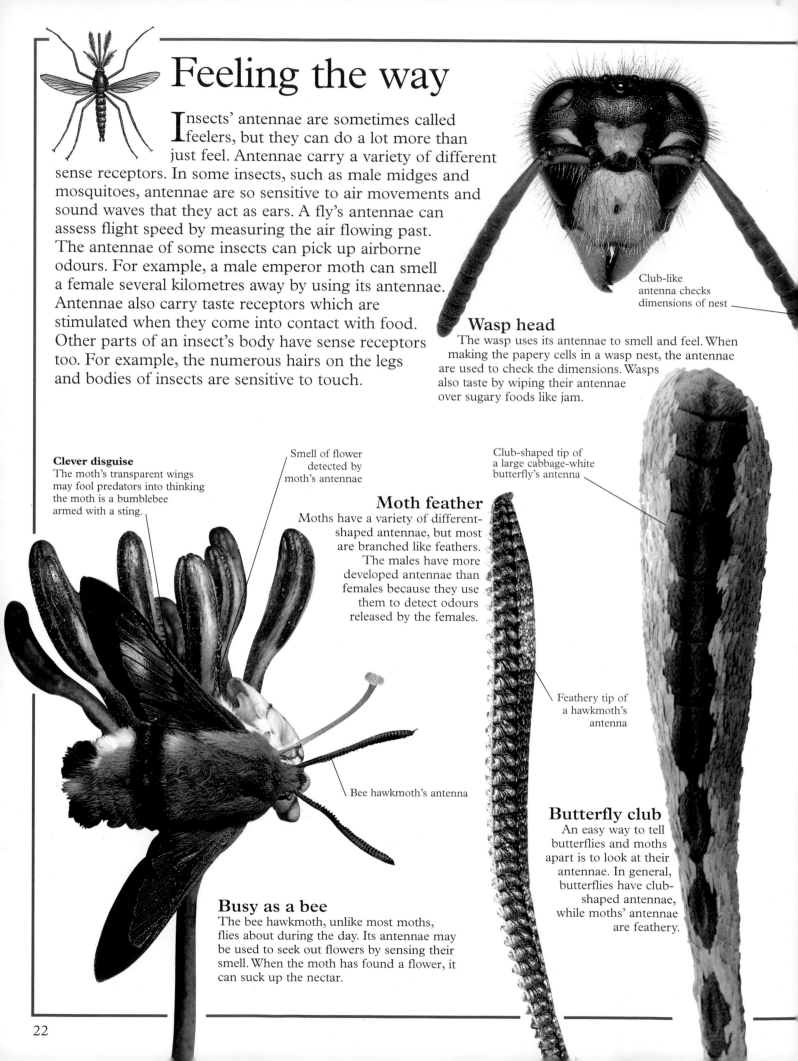

Feeling the way

Insects' antennae are sometimes called feelers, but they can do a lot more than just feel. Antennae carry a variety of different sense receptors. In some insects, such as male midges and mosquitoes, antennae are so sensitive to air movements and sound waves that they act as ears. A fly's antennae can assess flight speed by measuring the air flowing past. The antennae of some insects can pick up airborne odours. For example, a male emperor moth can smell a female several kilometres away by using its antennae. Antennae also carry taste receptors which are stimulated when they come into contact with food. Other parts of an insect's body have sense receptors too. For example, the numerous hairs on the legs and bodies of insects are sensitive to touch.

Club-like antenna checks dimensions of nest

Wasp head
The wasp uses its antennae to smell and feel. When making the papery cells in a wasp nest, the antennae are used to check the dimensions. Wasps also taste by wiping their antennae over sugary foods like jam.

Clever disguise
The moth's transparent wings may fool predators into thinking the moth is a bumblebee armed with a sting.

Smell of flower detected by moth's antennae

Club-shaped tip of a large cabbage-white butterfly's antenna

Moth feather
Moths have a variety of different-shaped antennae, but most are branched like feathers. The males have more developed antennae than females because they use them to detect odours released by the females.

Feathery tip of a hawkmoth's antenna

Bee hawkmoth's antenna

Busy as a bee
The bee hawkmoth, unlike most moths, flies about during the day. Its antennae may be used to seek out flowers by sensing their smell. When the moth has found a flower, it can suck up the nectar.

Butterfly club
An easy way to tell butterflies and moths apart is to look at their antennae. In general, butterflies have club-shaped antennae, while moths' antennae are feathery.

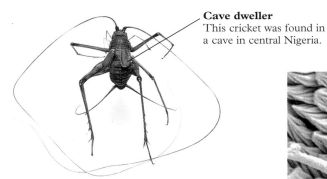

Cave dweller
This cricket was found in a cave in central Nigeria.

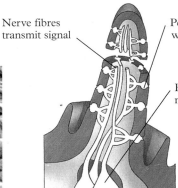

Nerve fibres transmit signal

Pore chamber where odours collect

Body of nerve cell

In the dark
The exceptionally long antennae of the cave cricket helps it to find its way inside dark caves. The antennae are sensitive to air currents and vibrations, and alert the cricket to other creatures moving about nearby.

A closer look
With higher magnification under the electron microscope, the sensory hairs of the large cabbage-white butterfly's antenna can be seen close-up. Two types of sensory hairs are visible.

Hair trigger
Certain setae (hairs) detect odours through a series of pores in their walls. The odours trigger nerve impulses. Male silkworm moths have as many as 3,000 pores on each sensory hair on their antennae. There are 17,000 of these hairs on each antenna, all devoted to picking up odours produced by the female.

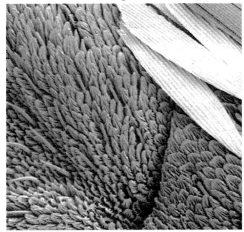

Bent antenna
Like the antennae of all weevils, this antenna is bent like an elbow and projects from the snout.

Sensory surface
By using an electron microscope, the sensory hairs and scales of a large cabbage-white butterfly's antenna are revealed. The hairs detect certain odours, such as the scent of flowers which the butterfly visits to feed on nectar. They also detect the odour of leaves on which the female lays her eggs. If the antennae are removed, the butterfly can still smell using its other receptors.

Sensitive hairs
The sensory hairs on the tip of the antenna come into contact with the surface of plants before a weevil feeds.

Bushy snouts
Male brush-snouted weevils use their bushy snouts to fence with other males when competing for females.

Plant probing
The brush-snouted weevil is a beetle with a long snout. It feeds on plants and the female lays its eggs in plant tissues, including freshly-fallen tree trunks, seeds, and nuts. By probing the plant surface with the ends of its antennae, the weevil picks up chemical clues.

Sound bugs

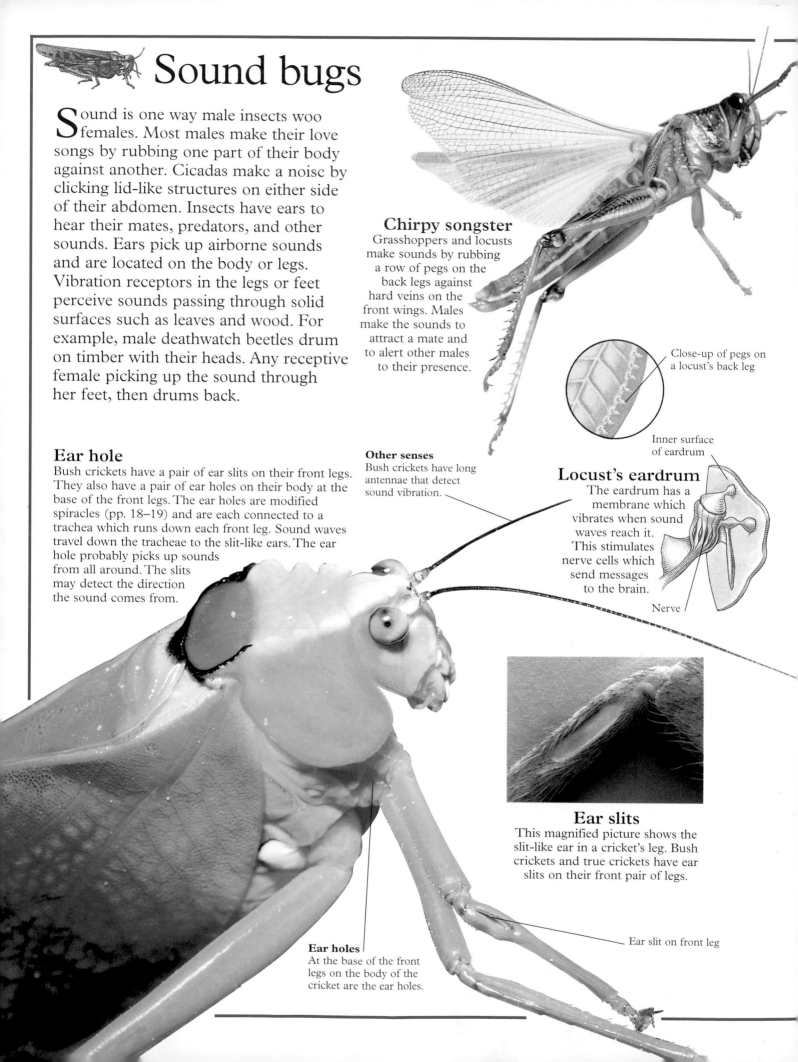

Sound is one way male insects woo females. Most males make their love songs by rubbing one part of their body against another. Cicadas make a noise by clicking lid-like structures on either side of their abdomen. Insects have ears to hear their mates, predators, and other sounds. Ears pick up airborne sounds and are located on the body or legs. Vibration receptors in the legs or feet perceive sounds passing through solid surfaces such as leaves and wood. For example, male deathwatch beetles drum on timber with their heads. Any receptive female picking up the sound through her feet, then drums back.

Chirpy songster

Grasshoppers and locusts make sounds by rubbing a row of pegs on the back legs against hard veins on the front wings. Males make the sounds to attract a mate and to alert other males to their presence.

Close-up of pegs on a locust's back leg

Inner surface of eardrum

Locust's eardrum

The eardrum has a membrane which vibrates when sound waves reach it. This stimulates nerve cells which send messages to the brain.

Nerve

Ear hole

Bush crickets have a pair of ear slits on their front legs. They also have a pair of ear holes on their body at the base of the front legs. The ear holes are modified spiracles (pp. 18–19) and are each connected to a trachea which runs down each front leg. Sound waves travel down the tracheae to the slit-like ears. The ear hole probably picks up sounds from all around. The slits may detect the direction the sound comes from.

Other senses
Bush crickets have long antennae that detect sound vibration.

Ear slits

This magnified picture shows the slit-like ear in a cricket's leg. Bush crickets and true crickets have ear slits on their front pair of legs.

Ear slit on front leg

Ear holes
At the base of the front legs on the body of the cricket are the ear holes.

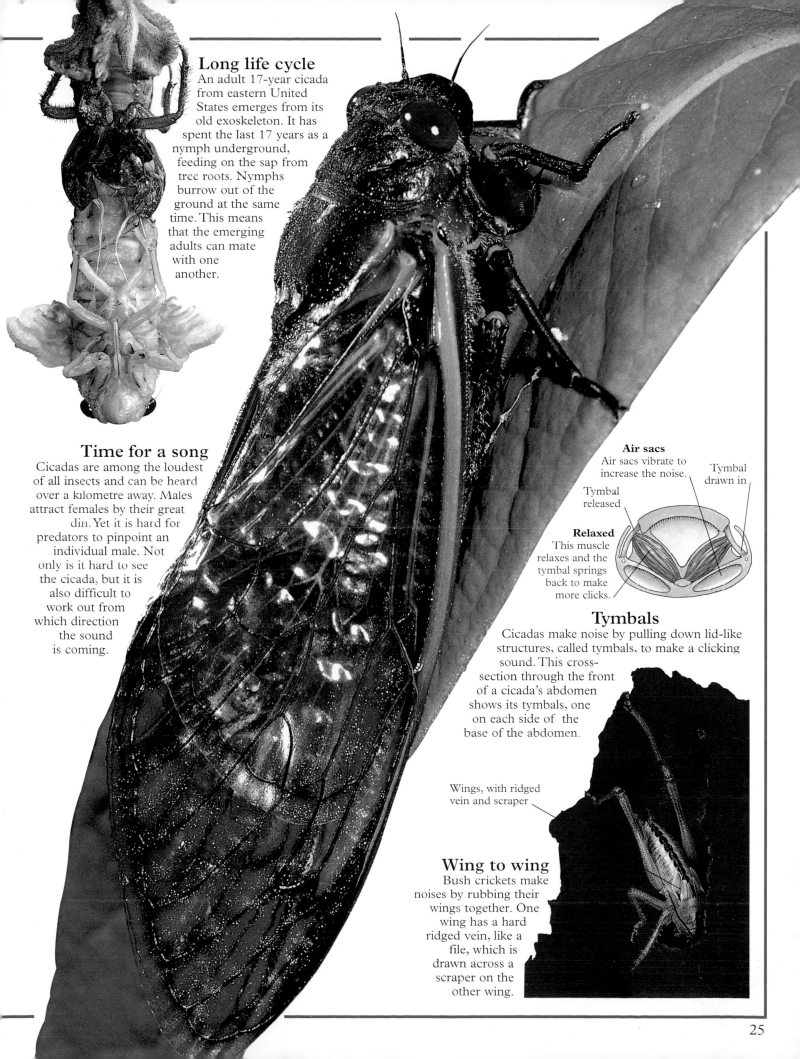

Long life cycle
An adult 17-year cicada from eastern United States emerges from its old exoskeleton. It has spent the last 17 years as a nymph underground, feeding on the sap from tree roots. Nymphs burrow out of the ground at the same time. This means that the emerging adults can mate with one another.

Time for a song
Cicadas are among the loudest of all insects and can be heard over a kilometre away. Males attract females by their great din. Yet it is hard for predators to pinpoint an individual male. Not only is it hard to see the cicada, but it is also difficult to work out from which direction the sound is coming.

Air sacs
Air sacs vibrate to increase the noise.

Tymbal drawn in

Tymbal released

Relaxed
This muscle relaxes and the tymbal springs back to make more clicks.

Tymbals
Cicadas make noise by pulling down lid-like structures, called tymbals, to make a clicking sound. This cross-section through the front of a cicada's abdomen shows its tymbals, one on each side of the base of the abdomen.

Wings, with ridged vein and scraper

Wing to wing
Bush crickets make noises by rubbing their wings together. One wing has a hard ridged vein, like a file, which is drawn across a scraper on the other wing.

Leg power

Inside an insect's slender legs are the muscles that make them bend. However, the muscles that provide the power for walking, running, or swimming are in the thorax. When walking and running, three of an insect's six legs are usually in contact with the ground at any one time. These form a stable tripod, with front and back legs on one side of the insect's body, and the middle leg on the other side, touching the ground. Insects can use their front legs for a number of different tasks. Praying mantises use their front legs for catching prey.

Many beetles have heavy body armour, but they can still walk, run, and fly.

Lining up
The praying mantis hunts other insects such as this juicy fly. By swaying from side to side, each of its eyes gets a clear view of the prey.

Juicy fly, still unaware of the mantis's presence

Folding leg
When at rest, the thin tip of the leg folds back. The mantis places this part of the leg on the ground when it walks.

Legs away
The mantis moves slowly forward and begins to unfold its front legs. The fly can take off in a split second. So the mantis has to be careful not to be seen until the fly is within reach.

Death trap
The fly is trapped between the sharp spikes on the mantis's front legs so there is no chance it can escape. Mantises sometimes bite off their prey's wings and legs and discard them before feasting on the body. The spiked legs can also be used against attackers.

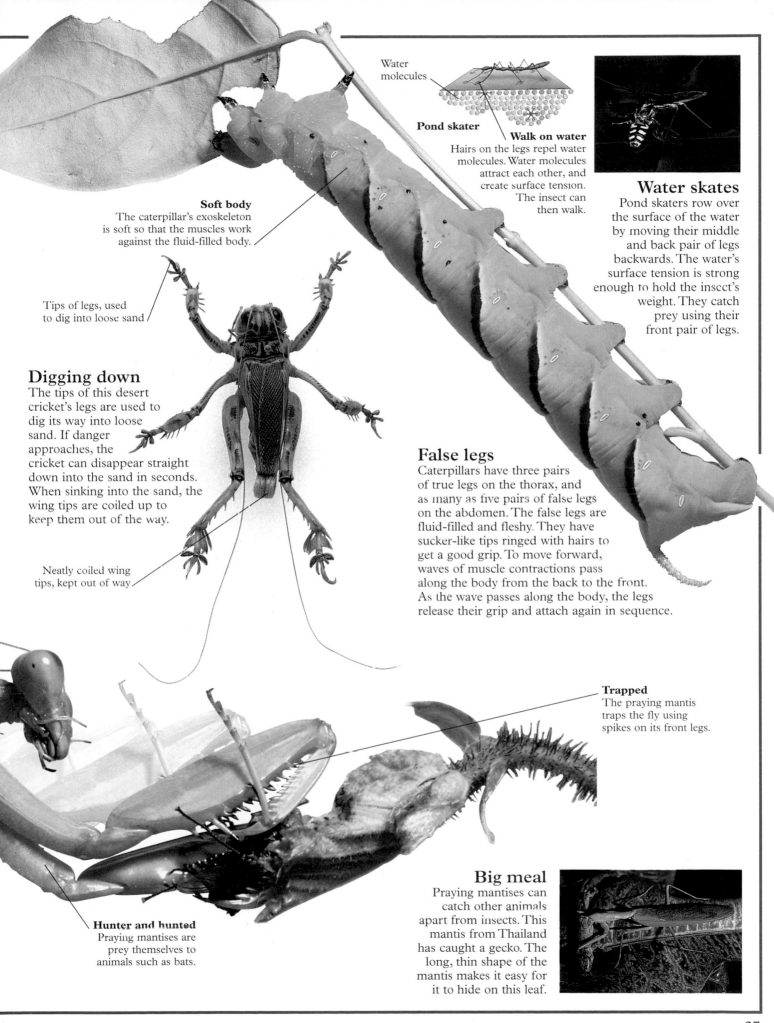

Water molecules

Pond skater

Walk on water
Hairs on the legs repel water molecules. Water molecules attract each other, and create surface tension. The insect can then walk.

Water skates
Pond skaters row over the surface of the water by moving their middle and back pair of legs backwards. The water's surface tension is strong enough to hold the insect's weight. They catch prey using their front pair of legs.

Soft body
The caterpillar's exoskeleton is soft so that the muscles work against the fluid-filled body.

Tips of legs, used to dig into loose sand

Digging down
The tips of this desert cricket's legs are used to dig its way into loose sand. If danger approaches, the cricket can disappear straight down into the sand in seconds. When sinking into the sand, the wing tips are coiled up to keep them out of the way.

Neatly coiled wing tips, kept out of way

False legs
Caterpillars have three pairs of true legs on the thorax, and as many as five pairs of false legs on the abdomen. The false legs are fluid-filled and fleshy. They have sucker-like tips ringed with hairs to get a good grip. To move forward, waves of muscle contractions pass along the body from the back to the front. As the wave passes along the body, the legs release their grip and attach again in sequence.

Trapped
The praying mantis traps the fly using spikes on its front legs.

Hunter and hunted
Praying mantises are prey themselves to animals such as bats.

Big meal
Praying mantises can catch other animals apart from insects. This mantis from Thailand has caught a gecko. The long, thin shape of the mantis makes it easy for it to hide on this leaf.

High jump

Sand flea
This may have got its name because it jumps like a flea. However, it is not an insect. It is a crustacean, like a crab.

When it comes to jumping, fleas are among the champions of their body size. These models show the cat flea jumping. The cat flea can leap 34 cm (13.39 in) high. This is at least 100 times its own body length. Fleas go on jumping until they find an animal from which to suck blood. They can jump hundreds of times each hour for several days. The key to this extraordinary feat is two pads of rubbery material, called resilin. These pads sit at the base of the flea's back legs. They are the remains of the wing hinges, present in the flea's winged ancestor. Resilin stores and releases energy.

Springtail
Springtails are tiny insects that live in the soil. They escape danger by flicking down their forked tails. When the tail hits the ground, the springtail is propelled into the air. At other times, the tail is held against the lower part of the body.

Back leg section

Catch engaged

Resilin pad depressed

Coxa

Femur

Trochanter

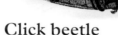

Click beetle
If you hold a click beetle upside down in your hand, it will bounce into the air with a click sound. The click mechanism is a peg and slot underneath the thorax. By curving the body, the peg is suddenly forced into the slot and the beetle is thrown upwards.

Preparing to jump
Energy is stored in the resilin pad by contractions of muscles in the thorax and the coxa, the first leg segment. When the leg is in this position, a catch on the edge of the body plates is engaged.

At an angle
Fleas usually take off at an angle, but can also jump almost vertically into the air.

1 As a flea gets ready to jump, it bends its back legs. The femur, third leg segment, is nearly vertical. Then the catch on the edge of the body plates is engaged. This prevents the release of energy stored in the resilin pad.

Coxa

Femur

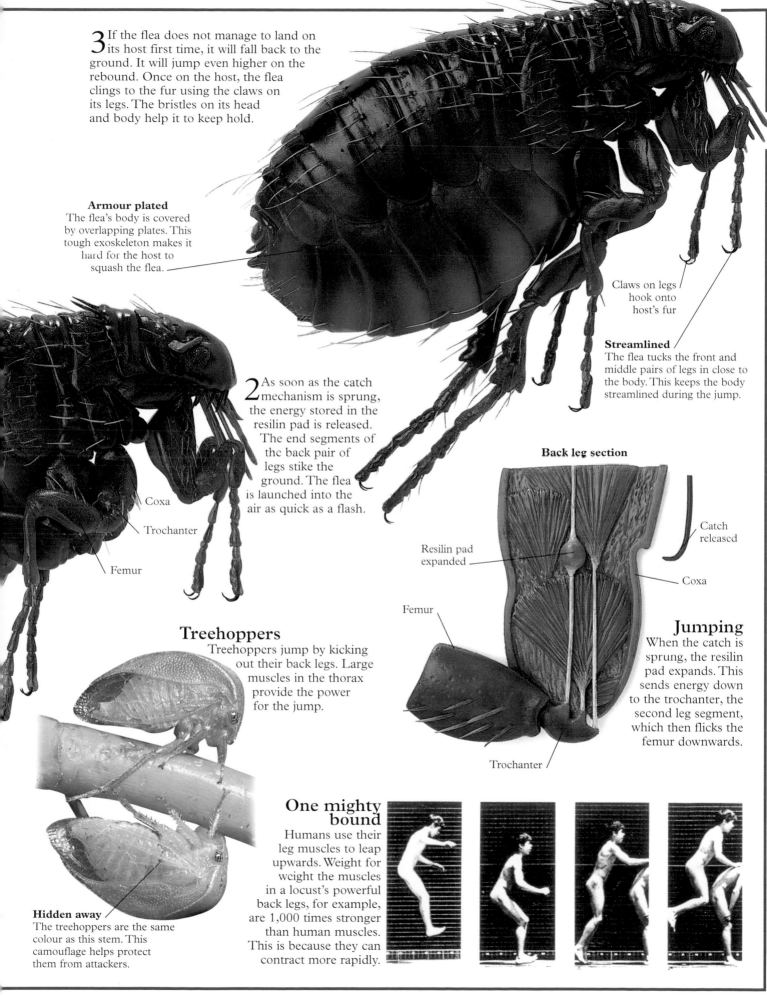

3 If the flea does not manage to land on its host first time, it will fall back to the ground. It will jump even higher on the rebound. Once on the host, the flea clings to the fur using the claws on its legs. The bristles on its head and body help it to keep hold.

Armour plated
The flea's body is covered by overlapping plates. This tough exoskeleton makes it hard for the host to squash the flea.

Claws on legs hook onto host's fur

Streamlined
The flea tucks the front and middle pairs of legs in close to the body. This keeps the body streamlined during the jump.

2 As soon as the catch mechanism is sprung, the energy stored in the resilin pad is released. The end segments of the back pair of legs stike the ground. The flea is launched into the air as quick as a flash.

Coxa

Trochanter

Femur

Back leg section

Resilin pad expanded

Catch released

Coxa

Femur

Trochanter

Jumping
When the catch is sprung, the resilin pad expands. This sends energy down to the trochanter, the second leg segment, which then flicks the femur downwards.

Treehoppers
Treehoppers jump by kicking out their back legs. Large muscles in the thorax provide the power for the jump.

Hidden away
The treehoppers are the same colour as this stem. This camouflage helps protect them from attackers.

One mighty bound
Humans use their leg muscles to leap upwards. Weight for weight the muscles in a locust's powerful back legs, for example, are 1,000 times stronger than human muscles. This is because they can contract more rapidly.

Taking flight

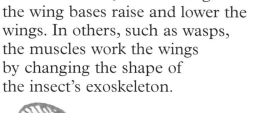

One of the key reasons for the success of insects is their ability to fly. Flying helps insects go in search of a mate, and to find new sources of food and places to live. Taking to the air is also a good way to escape predators. Insects were the first animals to fly, with winged insects appearing about 300 million years ago. All insects fly using muscles inside their thorax to power their wings. In some insects, such as dragonflies, the muscles attached directly to the wing bases raise and lower the wings. In others, such as wasps, the muscles work the wings by changing the shape of the insect's exoskeleton.

Hairy wings
Many insects have tiny hairs on their wings, like the hairs on this mosquito wing. Hairs on the wings of some insects smooth the flow of air, making it easier for the insect to fly.

Flying by
Once aloft, the lacewing continues to beat its wings up and down. The front pair of wings beat slightly ahead of the back pair.

Wing veins
Veins strengthen the wings and give them flexibility.

Launch of the lacewing
The lacewing lets go of its perch and starts beating its wings. On the first upstroke of the wings, the lacewing rises up into the air.

Ready to fly
To take off, moths and butterflies bring their wings down below their body. This reduces air pressure above them and they are sucked upwards.

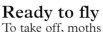

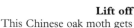

Lift off
This Chinese oak moth gets ready to take off by holding its wings together tightly.

On the turn
By angling the wings on one side, the lacewing can turn direction. These graceful insects are also able to fly in backward loops.

Bat food
Lacewings are not the best of flyers and tend to be blown about in air currents. Many lacewings fly at night when they are in danger of being caught by bats. Sometimes they can detect the high-pitched squeaks made by hunting bats, and take action to avoid being caught.

Sets of wings
Wasps have two pairs of wings. The back wings are linked to the front wings by a series of hooks. In flight, they act as one.

Wings up
The wasp moves its wings by changing the shape of part of the exoskeleton surrounding its thorax. When vertical muscles in the thorax contract, the upper part of the thorax is brought down. This raises the wings. In these models of a wasp, a contracted muscle is represented in red, and a relaxed muscle in blue.

Horizontal muscles relaxed

Vertical muscles contracted

Fancy wings
The lacewing's delicate wings are composed of sheets of chitin, the same material of which the exoskeleton is made.

Wing-hinges
Wasps' wing-hinges contain an elastic material called resilin.

Vertical muscles relaxed

Horizontal muscles contracted

Wings down
Horizontal muscles in the thorax contract to make the wasp's wings go down. Other muscles in the thorax act directly on the wing bases. These make subtle changes in the angle at which the wings are held.

Taking off
Many insects, such as the ichneumon wasp and the common wasp (below), use their legs to help launch themselves into the air. Insects can also make use of breezes to help them take off.

Bendy wing
The ichneumon wasp's front pair of wings can curve at their tips. This happens on the upstroke to give more lift when taking off.

Trailing legs
The wasp's long back pair of legs can help to launch it into the air. The legs trail out behind.

Top flyers
Dragonflies have outstanding powers of flight. This helps them catch their insect prey in the air. The dragonfly's two pairs of wings operate separately. In slow flight, the first pair beat slightly ahead of the second pair. When gliding or flying fast, the wings beat in unison.

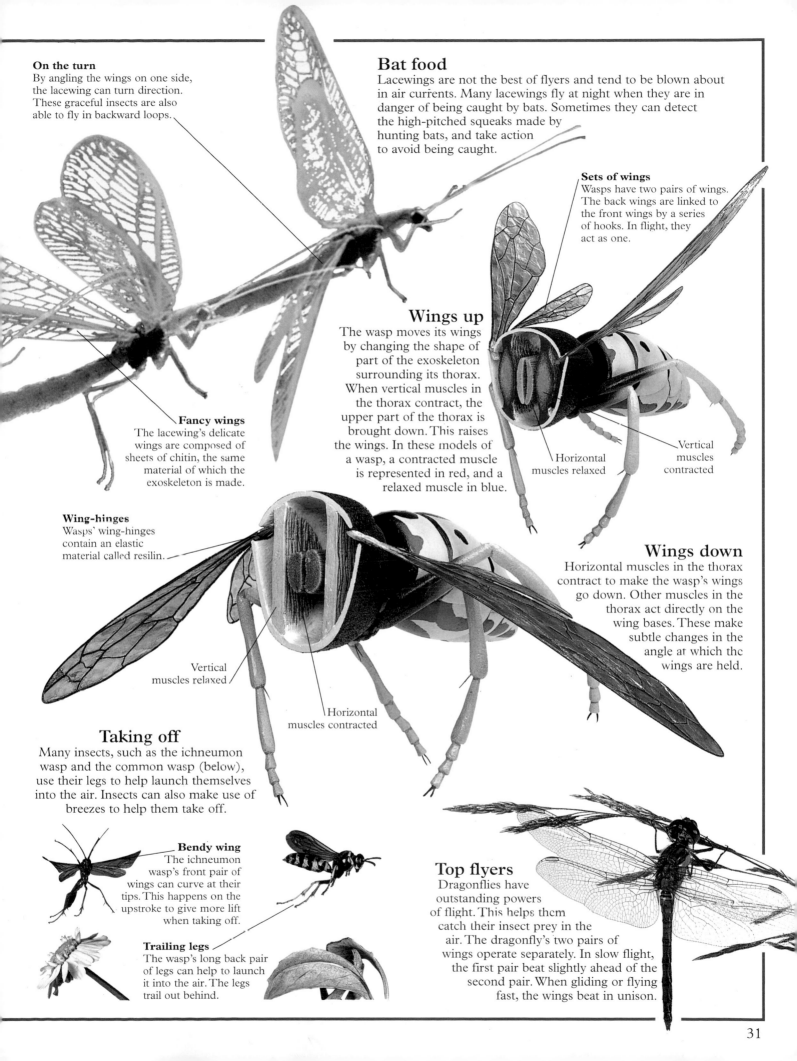

31

Unwelcome guests

Cuckoos lay their eggs in other birds' nests. These birds care for the chicks when they hatch.

No one likes to think of insects living on them, but for the human head louse, our heads make an ideal home. They need the warmth and shelter given by our hair, and the blood meals sucked from our scalps. They cannot survive for long if removed from the head. A heavy infestation of head lice can cause extreme itching. Fortunately, they do not transmit diseases, unlike the rarer human body-louse which sucks blood from people's bodies, and lives and lays its eggs on clothes. Insects can also harm people and other animals by feeding inside them. Plants can suffer from insects devouring the insides of their leaves, seeds, and other tissues.

Flying roach

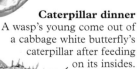

Cockroaches, like this monster, that live in kitchens are not keen on flying. Instead they scuttle about, slipping under counters and cupboards with ease.

Largest flying cockroach

Holes in lid of egg to let in air

1 Head lice eggs are known as nits. A female head louse lays up to 100 eggs in her lifetime. Each one is only 1 mm (0.039 in) long and is cemented to a strand of hair.

Nit closely attached to hair

Louse nymph
The young head louse, called a nymph, is a smaller version of the adult.

2 The head louse nymph forces off the lid of its egg by swallowing air to make its body become larger. Fluid also collects in the front of the body, making it bulge outwards.

New skin
The developing nymph's exoskeleton is shed along with the egg shell.

Thick wall
A tough egg shell protects the developing nymph.

Egg laying
The long egg-laying tube is inside a protective sheath, which is tipped with sense organs.

Parasitic wasp

Many kinds of small wasps lay their eggs in, or on, the young of other insects. When the grubs hatch, they feed on these young. Here, a wasp probes the surface of wood with her egg-laying tube to find a grub which is hiding inside.

Caterpillar dinner
A wasp's young come out of a cabbage white butterfly's caterpillar after feeding on its insides.

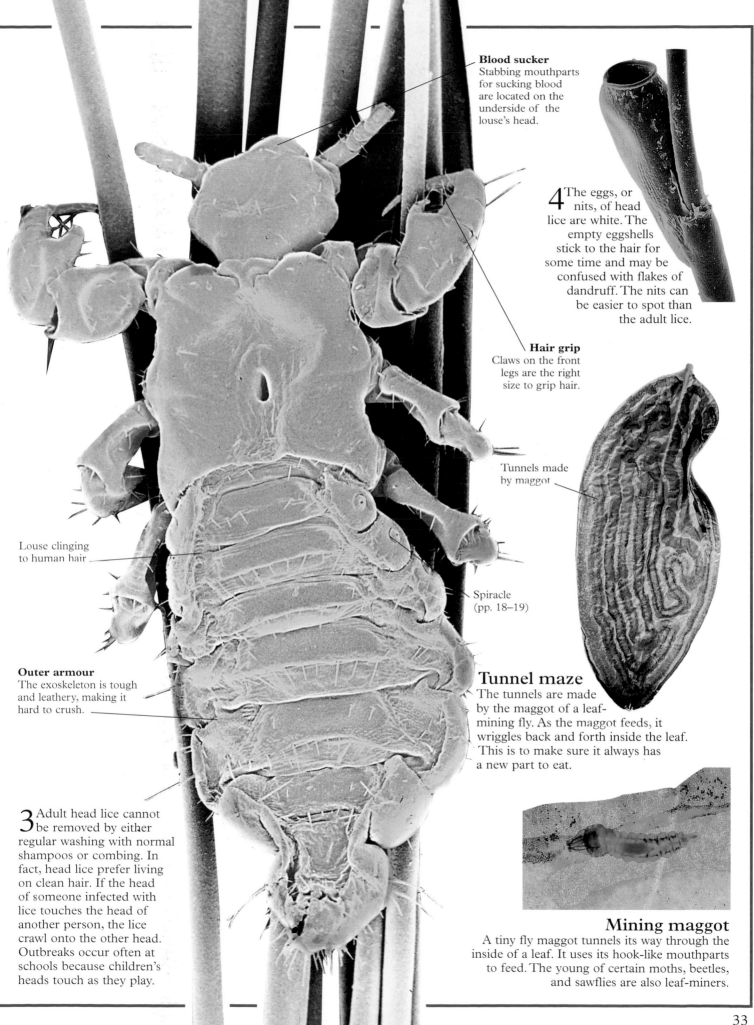

Blood sucker
Stabbing mouthparts for sucking blood are located on the underside of the louse's head.

4 The eggs, or nits, of head lice are white. The empty eggshells stick to the hair for some time and may be confused with flakes of dandruff. The nits can be easier to spot than the adult lice.

Hair grip
Claws on the front legs are the right size to grip hair.

Tunnels made by maggot

Louse clinging to human hair

Spiracle (pp. 18–19)

Outer armour
The exoskeleton is tough and leathery, making it hard to crush.

Tunnel maze
The tunnels are made by the maggot of a leaf-mining fly. As the maggot feeds, it wriggles back and forth inside the leaf. This is to make sure it always has a new part to eat.

3 Adult head lice cannot be removed by either regular washing with normal shampoos or combing. In fact, head lice prefer living on clean hair. If the head of someone infected with lice touches the head of another person, the lice crawl onto the other head. Outbreaks occur often at schools because children's heads touch as they play.

Mining maggot
A tiny fly maggot tunnels its way through the inside of a leaf. It uses its hook-like mouthparts to feed. The young of certain moths, beetles, and sawflies are also leaf-miners.

Nectar collector

One of the worker honeybee's many jobs is to collect nectar and pollen from flowers to feed the hive. The model below shows a worker honeybee pollinating a broom flower. The bee's long tongue unfolds to lap up nectar, which the bee then stores in its crop. As the bee probes the flower, pollen collects on its head, hairy body, and legs. Back at the hive, the pollen is mixed with a little honey and packed into wax cells. The nectar is passed from the bee's crop to be stored in wax cells. As bees forage, they pollinate flowers of the same kind by transferring pollen from one to the next.

Queen bee surrounded by worker bees

Petal eater
The earwig goes from one flower to the next eating petals. Pollen becomes attached to its body and is passed on to another flower, helping the flower to pollinate.

Well groomed
Each antenna is kept clean by passing it through a notch on the front leg.

Uncoiled
Butterflies are important pollinators of flowers. They suck up nectar through a long tube-like tongue, called a proboscis. The proboscis is coiled up when not in use.

Salivary glands
These glands in the head, and a pair in the thorax, produce saliva which helps dissolve the nectar.

Long tongue for sucking up nectar

Short mouthparts for sucking up blood

Spring blooms
As soon as the cold winter is over, bees come out to forage for food. They find nectar in the flowers that bloom early in the year, such as this crocus. They need to build up the hive's food reserves, which have been depleted during the winter.

Long tongue
This horsefly from Nepal has dual purpose mouthparts. It feeds on both blood and nectar.

Furry bee
The bumblebee has a lot of hair to keep it warm in the cool lands where it lives. It stores nectar and pollen in underground nests.

Worker head
The bee's glossa (tongue) is supported by other mouthparts when lapping up nectar. The mandibles have many uses. These include chewing pollen, moulding wax and plant resins, grooming, and fighting.

Salivary glands

Mandible

Antenna

Mouthparts to support the hairy tongue

Glossa

The crop
The crop expands to take in, at the most, 40 mg (0.0014 oz) of nectar. This is equivalent in volume to a pinprick of blood.

The valve
A valve, inside the gut, stops nectar passing from the crop into the midgut.

Rectum

Hairy face
Pollen grains sit wedged among the hairs on a worker honeybee's face.

Barbed sting

Pollen baskets
Pollen is collected on rows of hairs, called combs, on the inside of the back legs. It is transferred to pollen baskets on the outsides of the back legs.

Pollen combs
Pollen on combs on the left back leg is transferred to the basket on the right back leg.

Busy bees
When the bee returns to the hive, it regurgitates the nectar it has collected. The bee passes the nectar with its glossa to the other workers. They place the nectar in wax cells where it matures into honey.

Getting together

Mating means the chance of producing young. Some insects attract their mates by producing scents, singing, or offering gifts of food. For others, looks are important, such as wing colour in certain butterflies. Once the male and female are close together, touch can bring about mating. Many insects gather together in a swarm to mate, or meet where the female will lay her eggs. The males of most insects place sperm, or a package of sperm, directly inside the female. A few kinds of insects, such as springtails, put sperm packages on the ground, which the female picks up. Insect eggs are either fertilized by the sperm immediately, or the female can store the sperm for later use. A few insects, such as aphids, produce young without having to mate at all.

Many partners
Ladybirds may mate with several different partners, especially when there are many adults about.

Courting
Milkweed bugs often stroke each other's antennae before they mate.

Like a tortoise
Shield-like thorax and wing cases give the tortoise beetles their name.

Small males
Male insects are often smaller than females, as in this pair of tortoise beetles. The male beetle usually has to climb on top of the female to mate.

Great attraction
Male butterflies are often attracted by the female's wing size and colours. The females are attracted by scents produced by males. Some male scents encourage the female to land, so mating can take place.

Ovaries
Eggs are produced in the ovaries inside the female. They pass down a channel to the egg-laying chamber, during which time they are fertilized by the stored sperm.

Mating
When milkweed bugs mate, the male climbs on top of the female, with them both facing the same way. He begins to insert his sperm-transmitting organ, called the aedeagus, into her body. He climbs down and turns around, so the pair now face opposite directions. They stay in this position, shown in these models, for up to five hours, until sperm has reached a storage space inside her body. After they separate, both may go on to mate with others.

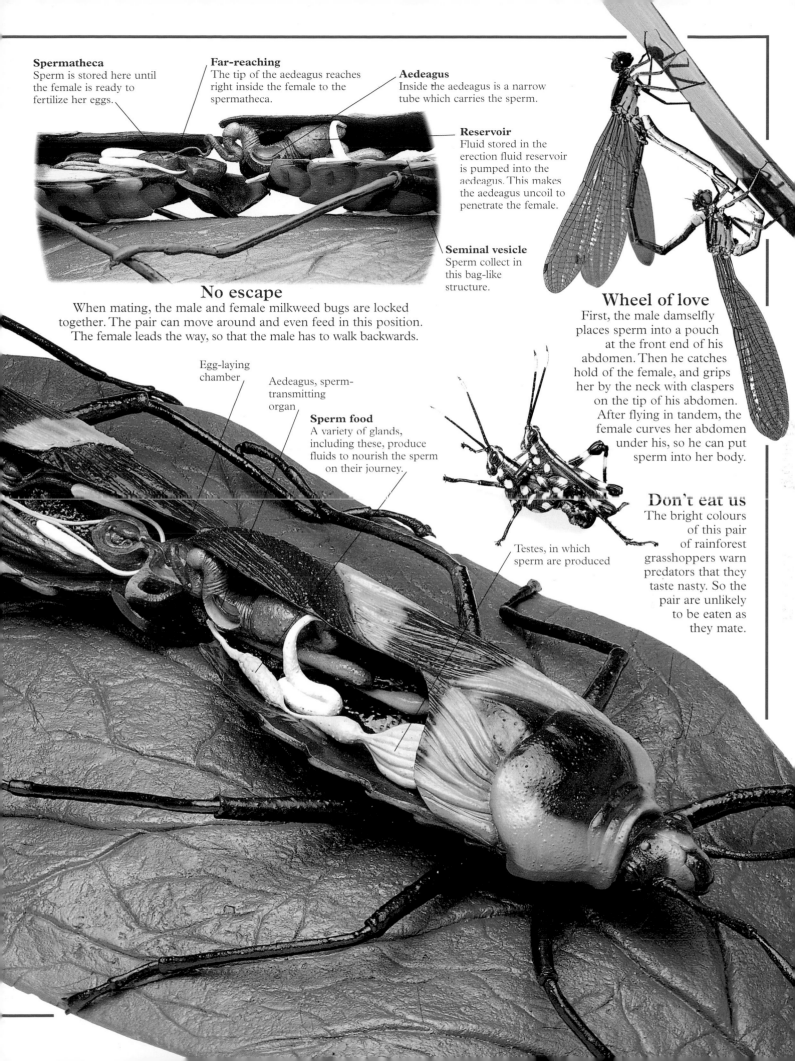

Spermatheca
Sperm is stored here until the female is ready to fertilize her eggs.

Far-reaching
The tip of the aedeagus reaches right inside the female to the spermatheca.

Aedeagus
Inside the aedeagus is a narrow tube which carries the sperm.

Reservoir
Fluid stored in the erection fluid reservoir is pumped into the aedeagus. This makes the aedeagus uncoil to penetrate the female.

Seminal vesicle
Sperm collect in this bag-like structure.

No escape
When mating, the male and female milkweed bugs are locked together. The pair can move around and even feed in this position. The female leads the way, so that the male has to walk backwards.

Egg-laying chamber

Aedeagus, sperm-transmitting organ

Sperm food
A variety of glands, including these, produce fluids to nourish the sperm on their journey.

Testes, in which sperm are produced

Wheel of love
First, the male damselfly places sperm into a pouch at the front end of his abdomen. Then he catches hold of the female, and grips her by the neck with claspers on the tip of his abdomen. After flying in tandem, the female curves her abdomen under his, so he can put sperm into her body.

Don't eat us
The bright colours of this pair of rainforest grasshoppers warn predators that they taste nasty. So the pair are unlikely to be eaten as they mate.

New life

Insects are careful where they lay their eggs. Many lay eggs on or near food, so when the eggs hatch, the young have plenty to eat. Eggs are also laid in places where they are less likely to be eaten themselves. They can be hidden under leaves or bark, and inside fruits or nuts. The eggs get some protection from their own shells, which also helps to keep in moisture. Some insects, such as cockroaches and praying mantises, provide extra protection by packing their eggs in a tough case. The most attentive insect parents stay with their eggs and young to defend them from attackers. A few kinds of insect, such as aphids, do not lay eggs at all, giving birth to live young instead.

Head emerging from hole made by mandibles

Mother care
A female stinkbug guards its precious batch of eggs from enemies who might find them a tasty snack. The stinkbugs often use their bodies as shields to protect their eggs from certain kinds of tiny wasps. These wasps try to lay an egg of their own inside the stinkbug's eggs. When the wasp grub hatches, it feeds on the bug's egg and destroys it.

On guard
This stinkbug is using its body to protect its eggs.

Bursting eggs
Insect eggshells are tough which makes it difficult for the young to hatch. Caterpillars, like this tobacco budworm caterpillar, use their mandibles (pp. 14–15) to chew a hole in the shell to escape. The young of some other insects pop out through a lid in the egg, or split it open along lines of weakness. Some young insects have special spines or teeth to help split the shell.

Foul-smelling
Stinkbugs also defend themselves from enemies by producing a foul-smelling substance from glands on the thorax, between the middle and back legs.

Eggshell
The eggs get some protection from their own shells. When the stinkbug nymphs hatch from the eggs, they will have exoskeletons to protect them.

Egg rows
The stinkbug's eggs are laid in tight rows around a plant stem.

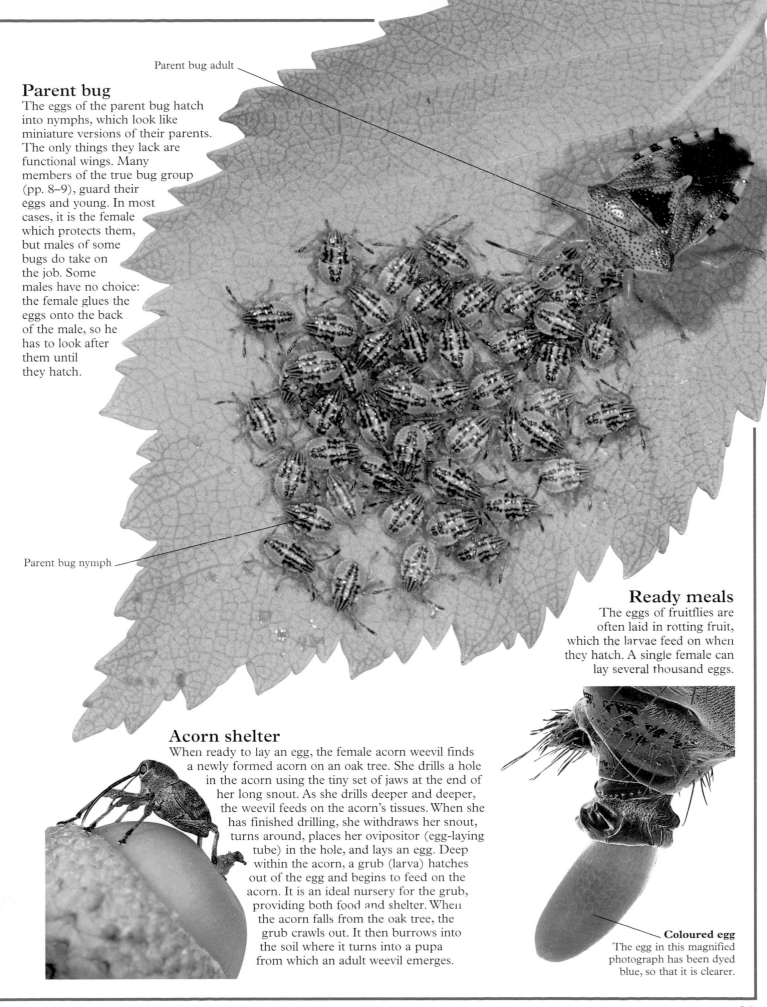

Parent bug

The eggs of the parent bug hatch into nymphs, which look like miniature versions of their parents. The only things they lack are functional wings. Many members of the true bug group (pp. 8–9), guard their eggs and young. In most cases, it is the female which protects them, but males of some bugs do take on the job. Some males have no choice: the female glues the eggs onto the back of the male, so he has to look after them until they hatch.

Parent bug adult

Parent bug nymph

Ready meals

The eggs of fruitflies are often laid in rotting fruit, which the larvae feed on when they hatch. A single female can lay several thousand eggs.

Acorn shelter

When ready to lay an egg, the female acorn weevil finds a newly formed acorn on an oak tree. She drills a hole in the acorn using the tiny set of jaws at the end of her long snout. As she drills deeper and deeper, the weevil feeds on the acorn's tissues. When she has finished drilling, she withdraws her snout, turns around, places her ovipositor (egg-laying tube) in the hole, and lays an egg. Deep within the acorn, a grub (larva) hatches out of the egg and begins to feed on the acorn. It is an ideal nursery for the grub, providing both food and shelter. When the acorn falls from the oak tree, the grub crawls out. It then burrows into the soil where it turns into a pupa from which an adult weevil emerges.

Coloured egg
The egg in this magnified photograph has been dyed blue, so that it is clearer.

Life changes

The young of some insects look like miniature versions of their parents. These are usually called nymphs. When nymphs first hatch out, they lack wings. As they go through a series of moults, they acquire wing pads before turning into fully winged adults. Other insects go through more drastic changes in their lives. They hatch out as young, such as caterpillars, maggots, and grubs, that are all called larvae. These look very different from their parents. The larvae grow bigger each time they moult. The fully grown larva turns into a pupa from which the adult emerges. Whether they start life as nymphs or larvae, adult insects do not grow because, unlike their young, they cannot shed their exoskeletons.

Pad of silk spun by caterpillar

Exoskeleton

Bird dropping
The caterpillar has a white streak running down its back. This makes it look like a bird dropping, and protects it from predators.

1 When the comma butterfly caterpillar is fully grown, it finds a twig or stem from which to hang. This is usually in dense vegetation, such as in a hedge. Wherever it settles, the caterpillar spins a pad of silk, attaching itself onto its support.

Chrysalis hanging from silken pads by hooks

2 The caterpillar has shed its soft exoskeleton for the last time to reveal the butterfly's pupal stage, called a chrysalis. The chrysalis hangs onto the silken pad by hooks at its tip.

Hardened surface of chrysalis

3 The surface of the chrysalis hardens to protect the adult developing inside. The chrysalis looks like a dead leaf, so as not to attract the attention of predators. The chrysalis stage lasts about 15 days.

Eyes with red pigment

Wings

Three pairs of legs

Wing width
The width of the wings can be seen more clearly in this side-angled view of the maggot.

Last stage
The transparent exoskeleton of the last maggot stage protects the pupa.

Fruitfly maggot
This picture shows the actual size of the fruitfly maggot.

Becoming a fly
Magnified images of the fruitfly maggot show its insides developing. The exoskeleton of the last stage of the fruitfly's maggot protects the pupa. Within this pupa, the maggot's body is almost completely transformed into an adult fly. Soon the fly will split open the protective case and begin its adult life.

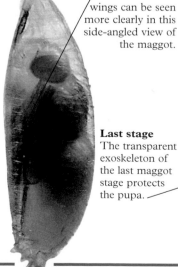

40

Changes within

The insides, as well as the outsides, of the butterfly change with each new stage. All the stages have a tubular heart along the top and nerve cord below. The reproductive organs (in red) develop to become functional in the adult stage.

Caterpillar
Caterpillars have a simple tube-like gut to digest the quantities of greenery they eat.

Chrysalis
In the chrysalis, the body is rearranged into that of the adult. The gut becomes coiled to cope with liquid food.

Adult
The reproductive organs are fully developed.

4 The chrysalis splits open and the butterfly pulls its body free. The butterfly's wings are still soft and wrinkled.

5 To fully extend the wings, blood is pumped through the vessels within the wing veins. The tube-like proboscis (pp. 16–17) is also extended by blood pressure. When the wings are dry, the butterfly will search for flowers from which to suck nectar. Depending on the time of year, the butterfly either seeks a mate, or if it is winter, finds a tree trunk to rest on.

Coiled proboscis

White comma
The white comma-shaped mark gives this butterfly its name and, for camouflage, resembles a hole in a leaf.

Balloon flight
The wing is like a bag that would expand into a balloon if it were not for tiny ligaments that hold the upper and lower membranes together.

Ragged wing
The ragged wing edges and brown outer surface help the butterfly blend in with dead leaves when resting.

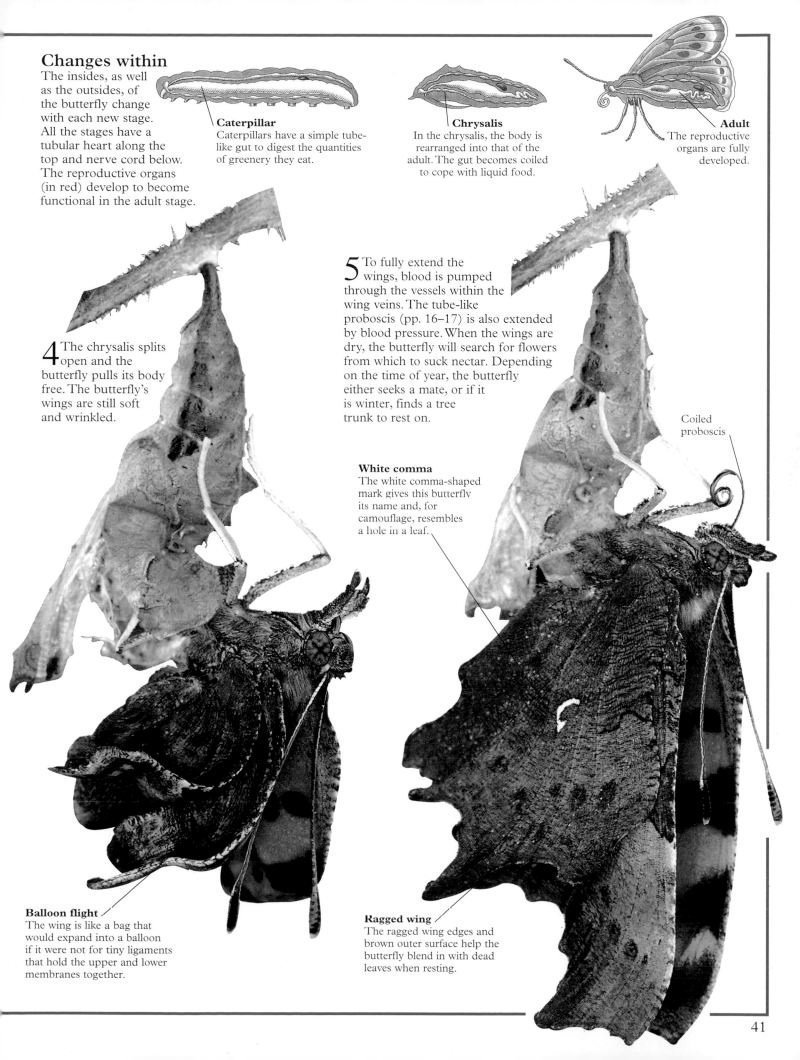

Glossary

A

Abdomen The insect divides into three regions: the head, the thorax, and the abdomen. The abdomen is at the rear of the insect.

Antennae All insects have one pair of antennae attached to the head. Antennae are segmented. They are covered with tiny sensory structures called setae. Antennae are used in various different ways, including smelling, tasting, feeling, and hearing.

The mouthparts of a mosquito

C

Camouflage How an insect blends in with its surroundings. For example, some butterflies and moths have wings that are coloured like leaves. Camouflage helps insects stay hidden from hungry predators. If the insect is a predator itself, such as a praying mantis, camouflage also helps it to remain unseen by its prey.

Chrysalis The name given to the pupa of a butterfly, inside which the adult develops fully. The chrysalis is protected by a hard, shell-like coat.

Colony A social grouping of a large number of the same insects – ants for example – that build and live in a community, dividing work according to specific tasks for the benefit of all.

Compound eye Insect's eye that is composed of separate light-sensitive eyelets called ommatidia. The number of ommatidia ranges from a few to several thousand. Some insects have huge compound eyes which give them amazing, all-around vision.

Coxa

Coxa The first segment of an insect's leg that extends from the thorax.

D

Diaphragm Elastic membrane that supports and separates the insect's heart from the blood-filled space containing the other body organs, such as the digestive and reproductive systems.

Digestion The process whereby food is broken down by the action of enzymes in the insect's gut into waste products and the various nutrients necessary for life.

E

Enzyme A substance produced by cells in an insect's digestive system, which helps in the chemical break down of food material.

Exoskeleton An insect's exoskeleton is an outer casing made up of layers containing chitin, a durable horny material. The exoskeleton supports and protects the insect's internal body organs. The insect's muscles are attached to the exoskeleton as are parts of the internal organs. The tracheae (breathing holes), for example, are connected to the exoskeleton at the spiracles (air holes).

Bee pollinating a flower

F

Femur The third leg segment of an insect which is connected to the trochanter.

G

Ganglia Nerve centres are made up of

Milkweed bugs mating on a leaf

two ganglia. Running through the insect's body is a row of ganglia linked together by a nerve cord. The ganglia receive signals from and pass on signals to different parts of the body. The ganglia in the thorax can control the movement of the insect's legs and wings directly, operating independently of the brain.

A flea jumping

H

Hindgut That part of the insect's digestive system located at the rear of the insect's abdomen, including the rectum and anus.

I

Insect An animal with a jointed exoskeleton, a body split into three parts (head, thorax, and abdomen), a pair of antennae, three pairs of legs, and one or two pairs of wings.

L

Larva One of the stages in the life cycle of an insect, such as a caterpillar, grub, or maggot. The larva hatches from an egg, and its main function is to feed and grow. Larvae (plural of larva) have simple mouthparts, and can have legs. Larvae increase gradually in size before becoming pupae.

M

Malpighian tubules Attached to the point where the midgut and the hindgut meet, these structures remove waste products from the

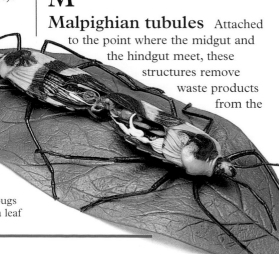

insect's blood. They work in a similar way to human kidneys. The waste products then pass into the insect's hindgut for removal from the body in its droppings.

Mandibles These are an insect's jaws. In insects with chewing mouthparts, they are broad with a cutting edge. In insects with piercing and sucking mouthparts, the mandibles are narrow and pointed.

N

Nectar A thick, sugary substance manufactured in the nectaries of flowers. Insects are enticed by the taste of the nectar, on which they feed. As an insect feeds, the flower's pollen sticks to its body and legs. The pollen is then transported to other flowers of the same species which the insect visits, resulting in successful pollination.

Nymph The term given to a young or immature insect whose life cycle does not involve a pupal stage. Nymphs hatch from eggs and gradually increase in size, developing wings and reproductive organs as they mature.

O

Ocelli As well as possessing compound eyes, insects have between one and three ocelli, or simple eyes. Ocelli can distinguish only varying amounts of light rather than actual images.

Ommatidia The scientific name for the eyelets or individual light-sensitive units of an insect's compound eye. Each ommatidium has a six-sided lens at the surface and extends back to the nerve cells connected to the brain.

Horsefly's compound eye

Ovipositor A tube-like structure at the tip of the female insect's abdomen which deposits fertilized eggs in a safe place for their development.

P

Palp One of a pair of sensory appendages belonging to the insect's mouthparts. Palps are used for touching and tasting food before an insect eats.

Parasite Animal, plant, or insect that lives and feeds in or on another, usually doing some harm.

Pollination The process by which many insects transfer pollen, a fine powdery substance, from one flower to another, so ensuring that seeds are produced.

Predator Animals (including certain insects) that hunt and eat other animals.

Wasp's wing mechanism

Proboscis An insect's long, tube-like mouthparts. In some flies, the proboscis channels saliva to the surface of the food. The semi-digested food is then sucked up through the proboscis.

Pupa The inactive stage in some insects' life cycles in which they transform into adults. The pupa of a butterfly is called a chrysalis.

R

Resilin A rubbery material found in insect wing hinges and in pads at the base of

a flea's back legs. The resilin stores and releases energy to enable the flea to jump.

S

Sense receptors Receptors on any part of an insect's head, body, or appendages which receive sensory stimuli, for example vibrations.

Setae Hairs on an insect's head, body, or appendages. Setae are extensions of the exoskeleton, and many are sensitive.

Spiracles Holes found along each side of an insect's body through which the insect takes in and expels air. The spiracles can be opened and closed to control the passage of air. The spiracles are connected to the tracheae (breathing tubes) inside the insect.

A single eyelet of the compound eye

T

Thorax The middle region of an insect's body. An insect's wings and legs are attached to the thorax.

Tracheae Inter-connecting breathing tubes throughout the insect's body. Air flows through the tubes, taking oxygen to the tissues. The tracheae are flexible so that they can expand and contract in order to take in and expel air through the spiracles.

Trochanter Section of an insect's leg located between the coxa and the femur.

Greenbottle fly

Index

Acknowledgements

Editorial assistance:
Julie Ferris and Nicki Waine

Design assistance:
Iain Morris and Jason Gonzalez

Additional photography:
Peter Chadwick, Gill Ellsbury, Frank Greenaway and Neil Fletcher

Photoshop retouching:
Bob Warner and Oblong Box

Thanks to:
John Brackenbury for editorial consultancy; Marion Dent for index

Illustrations:
12tr, 24cr, 25cr, 41tr Simone End; 23tr Michael Lamb

Picture credits
r=right, l=left, c=centre, t=top, a=above, b=below.

Ardea, London: John Clegg 17bc, JL Mason 28tr; **Biofotos / Heather Angel**: 34bl; **John Brackenbury**: 11br, 18tr, 25br, 33bl, bc, 34tr; **Bruce Coleman Collection**: Jane Burton 13tr, 40cr, c, cl, 41r, cl, John Cancalosi 2-3, 8c, 46-47, Eric Crichton 14cr, MPL Fogden 11tr, CB & DW Frith 27tr, Jeremy Grayson 36tr, Felix Labhardt 37tr, Andy Purcell 10bl, Dr Frieder Sauer 20br, Kim Taylor front cover bc, 14tr, 20bc, 27br, Carl Wallace 36bl, Peter Ward 13tl; **Microscopix**: Andrew Syred 19br, 21tr, tra, 22r, 23tc, cl, 24br, 40bl, br; **Natural History Museum, London**: 6cl, 11c; **Natural History Photographic Agency**: Anthony

Bannister 36cl, Stephen Dalton 13bl, 13br, Ron Fotheringham 30br, Peter Parks 16br; **Oxford Scientific Films**: GI Bernard 12bl, 14b, Michael Fogden 23b, David Fox 22bl, Avril Ramage 32br, James H Robinson 29bl, Kjell B Sandved 22bc, Tim Sheperd 39bl; **Animals Animals**: William D Griffin 25c, Raymond A Mendez 25tl; **Mantis Wildlife Films**: Jim Frazier 31cr, br, **Photo Researchers Inc**: Dawin Dale 20cl; **Planet Earth Pictures**: Jon & Alison Moran 11bc; **Premaphotos Wildlife**: KG Preston-Mafham 10cra, 17cr, 24bl, 28cra, 37cr, 38b; **Science Photo Library**: Dr Jeremy Burgess 14cl, 15br, 17br, 31l, 35cr, Dawin Dale front cover br, 20bl, Manfred Kage 14clb, Alfred Pasieka 10br, JC Revy 30cl, 30cr, Dave Roberts 12br, spine, David Scharf 14c, 16cl,

38tr, 39br, Cath Wadforth 31tr; **Science Pictures Limited**: 34cl.

Every effort has been made to trace the copyright holders. Dorling Kindersley apologises for any unintentional omissions and would be pleased, in such cases, to add an acknowledgement in future editions.